John Owen –
the man and his theology

John Owen (1616-1683)

John Owen –
the man and his theology

Papers read at the Conference
Of
The John Owen Centre for Theological Study
September 2000

Edited by
Robert W. Oliver

 EVANGELICAL PRESS

P&R
P U B L I S H I N G
P.O. BOX 817 • PHILLIPSBURG • NEW JERSEY 08865-0817

© Evangelical Press 2002
First published 2002

EVANGELICAL PRESS
Faverdale North Industrial Estate, Darlington DL3 OPH, England

e-mail: sales@evangelicalpress.org

web: http://www.evangelicalpress.org

British Library Cataloguing in Publication Data available

ISBN 0 85234 502 X

P&R PUBLISHING COMPANY
P.O. Box 817, Phillipsburg, New Jersey 08865-0817, USA

web: www.prpbooks.com

Library of Congress Cataloguing-in-Publication Data available

ISBN: 0-87552-674-8

Printed in the United States of America

CONTENTS

FOREWORD

The chapters of this book were originally delivered as papers at a symposium on the Life and Teaching of John Owen at the John Owen Centre for Theological Study in September 2000. The chapters are arranged in the order of the papers given and as is usual on such occasions the each contributor is responsible for the views expressed. It should be noted that Dr Ferguson's lecture 'John Owen and the Doctrine of the Holy Spirit' was the Martyn Lloyd-Jones Memorial Lecture which was included in the Conference in 2000.

The John Owen Centre for Theological Study was set up by the Board of the London Theological Seminary in 1999 to promote sound theology among the Evangelical Churches of this nation. It has been named after the great Puritan theologian John Owen who did so much of his important work in London. None of those involved in establishing this work would describe himself as an uncritical follower of John Owen.We do however profit from many of his achievements and admire the way in which he set about his task in the seventeenth century. In establishing the Study Centre in this capital city where Owen did much of his work and where rich resources are to hand for modern students we hope that we can encourage Christians to serve their generation as he did his. For this reason the Conference of 2000 was been convened to study aspects of his theology. To make the fruit of that occasion available to a wider public these papers are now published.

Robert W. Oliver
June 2002

Chapter One

JOHN OWEN (1616-1683) – HIS LIFE AND TIMES

Robert Oliver has served as a
pastor of the Old Baptist Church,
Bradford on Avon since 1971. Since
1989 he has lectured in Church
History and Historical Theology at the
London Theological Seminary and is
Adjunct Professor of Church History
of Westminster Seminary, Philadelphia.

I am going to him whom my soul hath loved, or rather hath loved me with an everlasting love; which is the whole ground of my consolation. The passage is very irksome and wearisome through strong pain of various sorts ... I am leaving the ship of the church in a storm, but while the great Pilot is in it the loss of a poore under rower will be inconsiderable.

Part of John Owen's last surviving letter, dictated to Charles Fleetwood on 22 August 1683.

JOHN OWEN (1616-1683) – HIS LIFE AND TIMES

John Owen's life from 1616 until 1683 spans one of the most momentous epochs in the history of these islands. He lived as a youth and young man in the reigns of James I and Charles I amongst social, political and religious tensions that strained society until it eventually erupted into the civil wars which culminated in the execution of Charles I. This was followed by the short-lived English republic. In a strange way John Owen was increasingly drawn into the company of the major agents of these remarkable events until he was playing his own part in them. The constitutional experiments of the middle years of the century proved unstable and in 1660 the monarchy was restored, harnessed a little, but backed by Laudian Anglicans who like the later Bourbons learned nothing and forgot nothing. With the Laudians in the saddle John Owen's life was redirected in a way painful at the time but to the eventual enrichment of the Church.

The Restoration ushered in penal times which have been described as the 'Great Persecution'. John Owen's prominence under Cromwell inevitably made him a target for the enemies of Puritanism. But although Charles II and his ministers tried marginalize Owen and his colleagues they eventually found that they had to do business with them. In fact Owen's personal prestige and the support of influential friends prevented him from suffering to the extent of many of his associates. Life was however always hazardous but repeatedly he used his influence for the welfare of his brethren.

I. Early Life

Some uncertainties surround John Owen's background. His father Henry Owen was Welsh and during John's student days at Oxford and later, he received income from a wealthy Welsh uncle. This was cut off when John's Parliamentary sympathies became evident in the conflicts of the 1640s. Of John's mother little is known.

At the time of his birth in 1616 his father was minister of the combined parishes of Stadhampton and Chiselhampton in South Oxfordshire. Henry Owen an Oxford graduate, had spent some years as a schoolmaster in Buckinghamshire before moving to the parsonage in Stadhampton. His parishes had a long-standing Puritan tradition supported by the patrons, the D'Oyley family. Many years later, John wrote,

> I was bred up from infancy under the care of my father, who was a Nonconformist all his days, and a pain-ful labourer in the vineyard of the Lord, so ever since I came to have any distinct knowledge of the things belonging to the worship of God, I have been fixed in judgement against that which I am calumniated withal.[1]

Before 1660 the term 'Nonconformist' described an Anglican clergy-man who ignored some of the rubrics of the Book of Common Prayer, thereby avoiding what he considered to be the remnants of 'popish superstition'. Requirements particularly obnoxious to the Puritans were the compulsory wearing of the surplice and making the sign of the cross in baptism. In the 1630s Archbishop Laud made further demands which included the railing in of the communion table at the east end of the church and bowing at the name of Jesus. Immediately after the Reformation the communion table had often been moved into the body of the church for the administration of the Lord's Supper. Laud's changes began to give the east end of the churches a more Romish appearance.

Laud's changes were still in the future when the young John Owen began his formal education under the supervision of his father in the Stadhampton parsonage. A solid foundation at home was followed by a short time at a school in Oxford before he was admitted to Queen's College, Oxford as an undergraduate at the age of twelve. His older brother, William was a student there at the same time. Both Owens graduated BA in 1632 and proceeded to their Master's degrees in 1635. At Queen's John's tutor was Thomas Barlow, an able scholar, but a trimming divine who was able to hold on to office through the many changes of the century. Owen however maintained a lifelong friendship with him. Shortly after receiving the degree of Master of Arts in 1635 Owen was ordained deacon by the Bishop of Oxford. He then began to read for his BD. This involved wide reading in English and Continental theology. Already he was being drawn to a close study of the Roman and Arminian controversies.

Life at Oxford came to an abrupt and unexpected end. In 1629 William Laud then Bishop of London was appointed Chancellor of the university. Laud, an Arminian, was bitterly opposed to the Puritanism in which Owen had been nurtured. His moves to introduce into the Church of England ceremonial unknown since the Reformation were increasingly repugnant to Owen. In 1633 Laud became Archbishop of Canterbury. He was now able to exert even greater pressure on the university to implement his policies. By 1637 Owen felt that he could stay no longer. He accepted a chaplaincy in the home of Sir Robert Dormer of Ascot, not far from Stadhampton. He did not however remain there for long, moving to the household of Lord Lovelace of Hurley, nearer to London. His employer seems to have found Owen's Puritan convictions congenial, but not his politics, for on the outbreak of Civil War in 1642 Lovelace declared for the king and Owen for Parliament. A break was inevitable and Owen moved to London, the Parliamentary capital and a centre for Puritan preaching.

Although Owen had accepted Puritan teaching and polity, he was in trouble spiritually. He was unsure of himself. It was one thing to have strong doctrinal convictions; it was quite another to be certain of his own position before God. An early biography states that he endured some five years of spiritual darkness. Andrew Thomson suggested that his *Exposition of Psalm 130* expressed some of the lessons learned in these years. It was in London that deliverance came. With a friend he went to St Mary Aldermanbury to hear Edmund Calamy one of the eminent preachers of the day. He was grieved to see an unknown country preacher mount the pulpit. His friend suggested moving on to another church, but Owen was too tired. To his amazement the unknown preacher's prayer gripped him. The sermon from Matthew 8:26, 'Why are ye fearful, O ye of little faith?' brought deliverance His bonds were broken, and he left the church assured of his everlasting salvation rejoicing in the love of God.

Like the young C. H. Spurgeon two hundred years later Owen was never able to discover the name of the preacher who had helped him. However with an assurance of his own salvation, Owen was prepared for a much wider usefulness. In 1642 he published his first work, *A Display of Arminianism* which challenged the thinking which had made such headway under Laud. He dedicated this book to 'The Lords and Gentlemen of the Committee for Religion' a Parliamentary committee for regulating religious affairs. In the summer of 1643 that Committee called upon Owen to take charge of the vacant parish of Fordham in Essex.

II. The Country Pastor

Fordham is a small village in the northern part of the county of Essex. It lay in the parliamentary heartland and probably for that reason its rector, who had been a chaplain to Archbishop Laud, deemed it expedient to leave. It fell therefore to the Parliamentary Committee for Religion to make temporary provision for the parishioners. Their choice was John Owen. A few months after his settlement, he married Mary Rooke from Coggeshall, a small town nearby. In Fordham Owen found himself faced with extensive ignorance of the gospel. In true Puritan fashion he visited from house to house and composed two catechisms for his people, one for young people and the other for adults. He also composed a small work, *The Duties of Pastors and People Distinguished.* This work which was a handbook for his people appeared early in his ministry at Fordham. Deeply suspicious of Laudian episcopacy, Owen was at first drawn towards the Presbyterians who were prominent in Parliament in the early 1640s. The *Duty of Pastors and People Distinguished* reflects his Presbyterian convictions. He expressed his disapproval of the Separatism which had been promoted by the Elizabethan Robert Browne and described Independency as 'democratical confusion'. However he soon applied himself to a more detailed consideration of church issues. Lacking the opportunity for personal discussion of the subject with an Independent theologian he made a careful study of *The Keys of the Kingdom of Heaven* by the New England Puritan, John Cotton. To his own surprise he found himself persuaded by Cotton, and forthwith aligned himself with the Independents eventually emerging as their greatest champion.

As a preacher his reputation was spreading. In April 1646 he was called upon to preach before the members of the House of Commons. Taking Acts 16:9, Paul's vision of the man from Macedonia, Owen urged the evangelisation of the neglected parts of the kingdom. He also pleaded for toleration in matters of religion. It should be remembered that some Presbyterians were pressing to establish a Presbyterian uniformity as rigid as the Laudian one which had so recently collapsed. In 1644 Samuel Rutherford published *The Due Right of Presbyteries* and followed this up with *The Divine Right of Church Government* in 1646, in both of which he attacked the extremes of Erastianism and Independency and also urged that the magistrate should suppress 'radical sectaries'. Freedom of conscience and worship were themes to which Owen would often return.

Just after his first sermon to the Commons Owen had to move from Fordham. The rector of Fordham for whom Owen was strictly a deputy had died and the living was now vacant. The patron of the parish wanted to exercise his right of appointment. At Coggeshall, a market town about five miles away from Fordham there was a vacancy occasioned by the removal of Obadiah Sedgewick to St Paul's Covent Garden. Owen was well known and the parishioners successfully petitioned the Earl of Warwick the patron for his appointment. Coggeshall had long enjoyed a Puritan ministry, which drew large congregations. So at the age of thirty Owen found himself ministering regularly to assemblies of about two thousand many of who showed great enthusiasm. He now set about applying congregational principles within the parish system. He preached to the large congregation, conducting the services according to the Directory of Public Worship approved by the Westminster Assembly. From that congregation he gathered a smaller church of those who had made a profession of faith and to these he administered the Lord's Supper.

III. The Emergence of a Leader

In 1647 while he was pastor of Coggeshall, Owen published his celebrated work on the atonement, *The Death of Death in the Death of Christ*. Although he was becoming known as Independent two Presbyterian members of the Westminster Assembly, Stanley Gower and Richard Byfield commended the work. Gower declared of Owen, 'The reverend and learned author of this book hath received strength from God (like another Samson) to pull down this rotten house [Arminianism] upon the head of those Philistines who would uphold it.'[2] The *Death of Death* clearly reflects Owen's study over many years and remains a classic treatment of the doctrine of particular redemption.

It was not simply as a scholar that Owen's reputation was growing. Charles I was now playing various factions off against each other. His perfidy provoked a second, brief, but bitter Civil War which eventually brought about his own ruin. During this War the Royalists seized Colchester, which was then besieged by Sir Thomas Fairfax, the Parliamentary commander who set up his headquarters at Coggeshall. Owen was invited to minister to the troops and became closely acquainted with the Fairfax and his deputy Henry Ireton. When Colchester was finally recaptured, it was Owen who was invited to preach at a thanksgiving service. By this time the army leaders were convinced that any agreement with Charles was impossible. His trial and execution followed.

The day after the execution Owen was called upon to preach before Parliament. He made no overt reference to the previous day's proceedings, but used the opportunity of a fast day to call for national repentance and reform. The crisis in church and state called for a programme of reform. Owen wanted some state recognition of Christianity, but a system flexible enough to allow participation by Independents as well as Presbyterians. At Coggeshall he had produced a working model of what was possible. Now from the pulpit of St Margaret's Westminster he encouraged his hearers to pursue a path never before pursued nationally. He urged reformation with the assurance that God will uphold those who are faithful to Him. In an appendix to the printed sermon he expounded his convictions that the state had a duty to make provision for the preaching of the gospel. This was entitled 'Of Toleration and the Duty of the Magistrate about Religion'. Here Owen expanded the views he had already expressed in 1646. He examined and dismissed arguments from Scripture for the physical punishment of heresy. He also argued that attempts to put down error by force had always failed. He challenged his critics,

> If errors must be tolerated, say some, then men may do what they please, without control. No means, it seems, must be used to reclaim them. But is gospel conviction no means? Hath the sword of discipline no edge? Is there no means of instruction in the New Testament established, but a prison and a halter? Are the hammer of the word and the sword of the Spirit, which in days of old broke the stubbornest mountains, and overcame the proudest nations, now quite useless? God forbid! Were the churches of Christ established according to his appointment, and the professors of the truth, so knit up 'in the unity of the Spirit and the bond of peace' as they ought to be, and were in the primitive times, I am persuaded that those despised instruments would quickly make the proudest heretic to tremble.[3]

Owen was not prepared to extend toleration to Roman Catholics, but here his reasons were political. He considered that the state should not allow freedom to subversive bodies. Referring the claims of popes to depose civil rulers, he noted,

Popish religion, warming in its very bowels a fatal engine against all magistracy amongst us, cannot upon our concessions plead for forbearance; it being a known and received maxim that the gospel of Christ clashes against no righteous ordinance of man.[4]

It was not long before the House of Commons sought Owen's services again. On 19th April 1649 he appeared before them, this time to preach from Hebrews 12:27. The removal of things that can be shaken included political and religious systems, all of which was brought about by the preaching of the gospel. The constitutions of the various European nations had been affected by their contact with Romanism. Owen saw the changes through which his own nation was passing as being a part of God's providential work in purging the various lands of popery. Turning to the Parliamentarians before him, he cried,

Give the Lord Jesus a throne in your hearts, or it will not be to your advantage that he hath a throne and a king-dom in the world. Perhaps you may see plenty of it, but not taste one morsel. Take first that which comes not by observation, – that which is within you, which is right-eousness, and peace and joy in the Holy Ghost'. Take it in its power and you will be the better enabled to observe it coming in its glory. Seek first this kingdom of God and the righteousness thereof, and all these things shall be added unto you'. Oh, that it were the will of God to put an end to all that pretended holiness, hypo-critical humiliation, self-interested religion, that have been among us, whereby we have flattered God with our lips, whilst our hearts have been far from him! Oh, that it might be the glory of this assembly, above all the assemblies of the world, that every ruler in it might be a sincere subject in the kingdom of the Lord Jesus![5]

This sermon had unexpected results. The next day Owen called on Fairfax and walking in the garden, met Oliver Cromwell, who came up to him and putting his hand on his shoulder, said, 'Sir, you are a person I must be acquainted with'. 'That', answered Owen, 'will be much more to my advantage than yours'. 'We shall soon see that', replied Cromwell, who pressed Owen to join him on his forthcoming Irish expedition.[6] He needed a chaplain who would be sympathetic to the Independents in the army and who would have the theological and pastoral skills needed to check some the extremists. He was also looking for a man with the spiritual insight and academic skills to advise on the needs of Trinity College Dublin. Owen was just the man.

Owen wanted to return to his pastoral work in Coggeshall and was reluctant, but Cromwell would accept no refusal. So leaving his family in Essex, Owen set out with the army in the summer of 1649. He was in Ireland from August until the following February. For much of that time he was unwell and this may explain the fact that he does not seem to have left Dublin, but lived in the castle while Cromwell campaigned in the countryside. Ill health did not lead to idleness. He inspected Trinity College, where he reported that the buildings were in need of repair and that there were very few teachers and students. Owen wanted to restore Trinity College to its intended role as a centre of Protestant learning in Ireland. While in Dublin he wrote, a small work *Of the Death of Christ*, defending objections made to his *Death of Death*. His greatest concern was however the spiritual needs of the people. He wrote of 'preaching to a numerous multitude of as thirsting a people after the gospel as ever I conversed withal'.[7] He returned to London to plead the cause of Ireland in a sermon before the House of Commons. 'Is it the sovereignty and interest of England that is alone to be there transacted? I could heartily rejoice, that innocent blood being expiated, the Irish might enjoy Ireland so long as the moon endureth, so that Jesus Christ might possess the Irish.' He pleaded with Parliament for a gospel ministry. 'I would that there were for the present one gospel preacher for every walled town in the English possession in Ireland.' Memories of Dublin pressed upon him,

> The tears and cries of the inhabitants of Dublin after the manifestations of Christ are ever in my view. If they were in the dark and loved to have it so, it might some-thing close a door upon the bowels of our compassion; but they cry out of their darkness and are ready to follow everyone whosoever, to have a candle. If their being gospelless move not our hearts, it is hoped that their importunate cries will disquiet our rest, and wrest help as a beggar doth an alms.[8]

Owen's return from Ireland preceded that of Cromwell and the army. In London, the Council appointed him 'Preacher at White-hall'. His duties included conducting opening devotions at Council meetings and preaching every Friday in the chapel of Whitehall palace. However Cromwell soon wanted him as chaplain on his Scottish expedition. Owen made two journeys north with the army between June and December 1650. Soon after his return from the second visit, the House of Commons voted that he be appointed Dean of Christ Church, the most prestigious of the Oxford Colleges. His close friend and colleague, Thomas Goodwin was already in the University as President of Magdalen. There were however complications. Edward Reynolds, a Presbyterian had been appointed to Christchurch in 1648, but was removed from office in 1650 because he could not take an oath of loyalty to the Commonwealth. Owen was reluctant to accept office. His most important work would be giving public lectures in theology and this prospect he dreaded. He had plenty of excuses.

[I] dreaded almost every academical employment, as being unequal to the task (for what could be expected from a man not far advanced in years, who had for several years been very full of employment, and accustomed only to the popular mode of speaking; who being altogether devoted to the investigation and explanation of the saving grace of God through Jesus Christ, had for some time taken leave of all scholastic studies; whose genius is by no means quick, and who had even forgot, in some measure, the portion of polite learning that he might have formerly acquired.[9]

His reluctance is understandable. He had left Oxford without completing his Bachelor of Divinity degree. He had been a country pastor and then an army chaplain and felt that he was no man for Christ Church Oxford.

IV. Oxford

Owen's objections were overruled and he returned to the university he had left fourteen years earlier. During the Civil War Oxford had been the royalist capital. The presence of a royal court and also a garrison had affected the university to the point that in the words of Peter Toon, 'The University had virtually ceased to exist as a centre of learning.'[10] Some progress had been made in the restoration of study, but much remained to be done. In 1652 Cromwell was appointed Chancellor of the University and he appointed Owen as his Vice Chancellor with responsibility for the administration. Owen held this position until 1657. He proved to be a good administrator and a firm disciplinarian.

Throughout these years there remained considerable sympathy for Anglicanism and indeed the royalist cause at

Oxford. Owen had to live with this and turned a blind eye to the Prayer Book services in at least one college chapel. He was also fighting a battle with radical sectarianism in the country. In the army and also in one Protectorate Parliament there were demands for the abolition of the universities. Some radicals insisted that academic studies played no part in ministerial preparation. Owen resisted these demands when he spoke on behalf of the University and also when preaching in London. The radicals demanded the abolition of degrees in divinity and the wearing of academic dress. On these two matters Owen may not have had strong convictions, but he had no doubt about the importance of university education to serve the needs of Church and State. Perhaps to bring its Puritan Vice Chancellor into line the conservative University Convocation conferred upon him and his friend Thomas Goodwin the degree of Doctor of Divinity in 1653.

In 1657 Richard Cromwell was appointed Chancellor and nominated his own vice Chancellor. At the installation of his successor, Owen gave a report of his stewardship. After recording the number of degrees awarded, he continued,

> Professors' salaries, lost for many years, have been maintained and paid; many offices, by no means negligible ones sustained; the rights and privileges of the University have been defended against some efforts of its enemies; the treasury is tenfold increased; many of every rank in the university have been promoted to various honours and benefices; new exercises have been introduced and established; old ones have been duly performed; reformation of manners has been diligently undertaken in spite of the grumbling of certain profligate brawlers; labours have been numberless.[11]

A later Chancellor, Edward Hyde, Lord Clarendon, a bitter opponent of Puritanism later admitted that the Oxford of Owen's time 'yielded a harvest of extraordinary good and sound knowledge in all parts of learning'.[12] Owen continued at Oxford as Dean of Christ Church until March 1660. He regretted later that at Oxford he had not been able to write as much as he had hoped. He did however publish *De Iustitia* a work on the justice of God. Another product of these years was his *Theologouma Pantodapa,* not published until after he left the University in 1661. This contains the substance of theology lectures given at Oxford. It remained generally inaccessible in Latin until recently translated by Dr Stephen Westcott and published in 1994 under the title, *Biblical Theology.*[13] Owen's preaching in these years should be noted. From 1652 to 1657 Owen and Goodwin alternated as Sunday preachers in the University Church. Some of his sermons preached to undergraduates in these years have survived as his treatises on *Mortification* and *Temptation.* He also revised and published sermons on *Communion with God,* originally preached at Coggeshall and possibly repeated in the University. Anthony Wood who had little sympathy with Puritanism left an interesting description of Owen the preacher,

> his personage was proper and comely and he had a very graceful behaviour in the pulpit, an eloquent elocution, a winning and insinuating deportment and could by the persuasion of his oratory ... move and win the affections of his admiring auditory almost as he pleased[14]

There is some mystery as to Owen's church membership in these years. He was accepted as an Independent in good standing and took a prominent part in the Savoy Assembly which met to deal with important issues among these churches. It is known that Thomas Goodwin established a gathered church at

Magdalen College, but Owen's name does not appear on the list of members. It has been suggested that Owen sought to establish such a church at Christ Church but no evidence for this is known. Peter Toon mentions another alternative and that is that he may have established a church at Stadhampton, where he had a house. Andrew Thomson reports a tradition that he held services there when he was not preaching in Oxford. Certainly he held services in Stadhampton from 1660 to 1662. Whatever may have happened after 1660 it is difficult to imagine that Owen who had plenty to do in Oxford and was often in London would have had time to care for a church at Stadhampton during his years at Christ Church.

Owen was often called to London in these years. Cromwell valued his counsel and he was often called upon to preach before Parliament. He was deeply involved in discussions about the settlement of religion. He did not want to see the abolition of the parish system or of tithes. He had already demonstrated at Coggeshall that the parish church could be a preaching place or a centre of evangel-ism and that along side there could exist a gathered church composed of those who professed faith in Christ and who would accept the obligations of mutual care and discipline. This system he wanted to see extended to the whole country. There was an ecclesiastical vacuum in the 1650s. The Presbyterian system envisaged by the Westminster Assembly had never been established across England and Wales. An amazing variety of sectarian movements were spreading. Owen believed that these must be faced by faithful preaching. Eventually Cromwell's government set up a Board of thirty-eight Commissioners or Triers of whom Owen was one. They were to examine candidates to serve in the parish churches and to approve only men of known godliness and abilities. In practice they approved Independents, Presbyterians and Baptists. Baxter believed that their enquiries were too rigorous. They were too fearful of Arminianism and too particular in enquiring for evidences of sanctification, but he admitted that 'so great was the benefit above the hurt, which they brought to the Church that many thousands of souls blest God for the faithful ministers whom they let in and grieved when the prelatists afterwards [between 1660 and 1662] cast them out again'.[15]

From 1656 it was evident that Owen was no longer so powerful a figure in the Protector's court. Cromwell was under pressure to accept the crown and Owen opposed this. In the end Cromwell himself decided against acceptance, but Owen never seems to have been so close to him again. Cromwell himself died on 3rd September 1658. Shortly before his death he had nominated his son Richard as his successor as Protector. Richard proved incapable of governing the country. There was a period of growing uncertainty before General Monck at the head of an army from Scotland stepped in to restore order and a series of moves led to the restoration of the monarchy in the Spring of 1662. Before that happened Owen played a leading part in a major development for the Congregational churches.

The Congregational Independents were multiplying throughout the 1650s. A number of their leaders had risen to prominence in government. Unlike the Presbyterians or the Baptists they had no nationally recognised statement of faith. There was also a need for some consolidation of their position. They explained in words most probably written by Owen,

> the generality of our churches have been in a manner like so many ships, though holding forth the same general colours, launched singly, and sailing apart and alone on the vast ocean of these tumultuous times, and exposed to every wind of doctrine, under no other conduct than that of the Word and the Spirit, and their particular elders and principal brethren, without association among themselves, or as much as holding out common lights to others, whereby to know where they were.[16]

Cromwell saw an Independent Synod as a potential source of trouble, but eventually was persuaded that such a meeting should be assembled. In the summer of 1658 arrangements were made for a national Synod of Independents to meet at the Savoy Palace in London in September. Unlike the Westminster Assembly this meeting was not summoned by Parliament, but curiously the letter making arrangements for a preliminary meeting was sent out by Henry Scobell, clerk to the Council of State. Before the representatives of the churches could assemble Oliver Cromwell died.

At the Synod it was agreed to make a revision of the Westminster Confession for the Independent Churches. The work was committed to Thomas Goodwin, Philip Nye, William Bridge, Joseph Caryl, William Greenhill and John Owen, all of whom with the exception of Owen had been members of the Westminster Assembly. The Westminster Confession was lightly revised to take account of Independent convictions on Church government and a new chapter 20 added, 'On the Gospel and the Extent of the Grace thereof'. It concluded with a new chapter of 30 sections on Independent church order. It is generally believed that Owen wrote the preface to this confession which has become known as *The Savoy Declaration of Faith and Order.* Williston Walker, (1860 –1922) a later Congregational historian was disparaging about the Declaration's lack of originality and described the preface as long and dreary, but conceded that it advocated an unusual spirit of toleration. Dreary or not it provides useful information about the way in which the revisers worked. The Synod certainly was marked by a spirit of love and unity and indeed something of this ethos was known among Christian people generally. Philip Henry noted this, 'There was a great change in the tempers of good people throughout the nation, and a mighty tendency to peace and unity, as if they were by consent weary of their long clashings.'[17]

Future events may have been casting their shadows ahead. It was a time for believers to learn lessons. Even as the Synod was meeting events were moving rapidly. Oliver Cromwell's son Richard succeeded his father as Lord Protector and was believed to favour Presbyterianism. A Parliament was summoned for January 1659 and Owen was called to preach before it on a fast day in February. Something of the national uncertainty can be sensed from the sermon. Owen argued that all the gains of the previous few years were as the result of faith and prayer. He detected dangerous tendencies the country,

> Do you not know that if the former profane principle should prove predominant in this nation, that it will quickly return to its former station and condition, and that with the price of your dearest blood? And yet is there not already such a visible prevalency of it, that in many places the very profession of religion is become a scorn; and in others those old forms and ways taken up with greediness, which are a badge of apostasy from all former engagements and actings.[18]

Trouble was indeed brewing. Parliament was factious and lacked good leadership. The army was restless, the soldiers' pay was in arrears. Owen was seldom in Oxford at this time. He seems to have spent a great deal of energy trying to heal divisions among leading men in London. Early in 1659 he formed a church there. It members included Lords Fleetwood and Desborough, both prominent army officers, who were viewed with suspicion by Richard Cromwell. Cromwell tried to disband the army officers' council, but Fleetwood and Desborough refused to co-operate. The officers persuaded Richard to recall the so-called 'Rump', a remnant of the last Parliament to have been summoned by Charles I. Although Owen seems to have felt that this move was preferable to the inertia which paralysed the government such a recall inevitably cast a doubt over all the legitimacy of recent constitutional developments. About 160 members returned and Owen preached to them. Soon after this Richard Cromwell retired into private life. It is difficult to know exactly what part Owen took in this high political drama. He was certainly very close to the major players. Baxter was very critical of him. 'Dr Owen and his assistants did the maine work: his high spirit thought the place of Vicechancellor & Dean of Christ's Church to be too low: and if the Protector will not do as he would have him, he shall be no Protector'. Referring to the church Owen had formed and to which a number of important army officers belonged, he wrote tartly, 'This church-gathering hath bin the church-scattering project.'[19]

The Rump achieved very little and was soon dissolved by the army grandees. Into the political and constitutional vacuum moved General Monck the army commander in Scotland with his forces. He once again restored an older body consisting of the Rump together with MPs who had survived earlier expulsions. There was by now a Presbyterian majority. Within a few months this Parliament dismissed Owen from his position at Christ Church and restored Edward Reynolds replaced by Owen so many years earlier.

Owen retired to Stadhampton with his family and began to hold services in his house. Here he would receive news from London. Already moves were being made to restore Charles II who was ready to 'promise a liberty to tender consciences'. Presbyterians were hoping to be incorporated within a restored Church of England. Episcopacy would have to be accepted, but hints were being made of concessions to Puritans. Several Presbyterians including Richard Baxter accepted royal chaplaincies. From his Oxfordshire village Owen knew that the Cromwellian Church Settlement could not last much longer. The great question was how much religious freedom would be possible. Presbyterians with high hopes of comprehension within a modified Church of England joined in discussions with the Anglican leaders in the Savoy Conference in the Spring of 1661.

The Conference was already running into difficulties when a general election dashed all hopes of success. The so-called Cavalier Parliament which assembled in May 1661 represented a victory for royalism and the restoration of Laudian episcopacy. By the end of the year the Corporation Act excluded from municipal bodies all who refused to renounce the Solemn League and Covenant, to take the sacrament according to the rites of the Church of England or to swear not to resist the king. In April 1662 a revised Prayer Book was promulgated and in May Parliament passed an Act of Uniformity which insisted total acceptance of this book by all clergy or forfeiture of their livings. The result was the Great Ejection on Black Bartholomew's Day 1662 when almost 2000 Puritan Clergy were expelled from their benefices.

In a small work, *A Discourse Concerning Liturgies,* Owen explained why he could not subscribe to the demands of the Act of Uniformity. He argued that in the first three hundred years of the Christian era liturgies were unknown and the churches enjoyed union 'and the uniformity in worship which Christ requires observed among them … which makes the case most deplorable, that it should now be made the hinge whereon the whole exercise of the ministry must turn.'[20] Owen explained that he did not object to the use of a lectionary or general requirements for the order of worship, but to 'the composing of forms of prayer in the worship of God, in all gospel administrations, to be used by all ministers of the churches, in all public assemblies, by a precise reading of the words prescribed unto them, with commands for the reading of other things, which they are not to omit, upon the penalty of the sanction contained in the sanction of the whole service and the several parts of it'.[21]

V. Leadership in the Storm

Owen had been removed from his position at Oxford before
Black Bartholomew Day and for a time remained at
Stadhampton, where many old colleagues and friends called
for consultation. There also he quietly continued worship in his
house. Technically this was illegal, although the Conventicle Act
was not passed until 1664. Already the justices of Bedford had
put John Bunyan in jail under the terms of an act dating from
1593. The Oxfordshire justices may have been wary of instituting
proceedings against the former Vice Chancellor of the
University and in any case the D'Oyley family, powerful land
owners around Stadhampton were Puritan in sympathy. During
these early years Owen had at least two interviews with Lord
Chancellor Clarendon, popularly regarded as the moving spirit
behind the anti-Puritan legislation, soon to be dubbed the
'Clarendon Code'. Clarendon told Owen that he must not
preach, but urged him to employ his talents writing something
against the Roman Catholics. Owen was to do both. The future
in England was dark. He received approaches from abroad.
Dutch universities were interested, as was the Congregational
Church in Boston Massachusetts, where the great John Cotton
had earlier ministered. Owen was however convinced that his
duty was in Old England. Soon after the passing of the
Conventicle Act in 1664, Owen's house was raided and he was
caught preaching to thirty or more people. Probably before this
Owen had sent his wife and children to Stoke Newington where
they stayed in the house of Charles Fleetwood, one of
Cromwell's old generals. Owen himself seems to have decided
to move to London after his prosecution. Both Owen and Goodwin were taking opportunities to preach in the capital in these
years.

   In the mid 1660s the nation was hit by a series of disasters.
In 1665 the Great Plague, Britain's last major outbreak of
bubonic plague scourged the capital. King and Parliament fled

from London, as did many of the clergy of the Established Church. A number of the ejected Puritan ministers took the opportunity to minister to their old flocks, some even from their old parish church pulpits. From the safety of Oxford Parliament struck, passing the Five Mile or Oxford Act, which forbade Nonconformist ministers to live or visit places where they had previously ministered, or reside in any corporate town. The next year 1666 was the year of the Great Fire of London and in its wake nonconformists showed greater boldness in meeting for worship. The culminating disaster was defeat at the hands of the Dutch in 1667. The Dutch sent their vessels up the Firth of Forth and then in an even bolder stroke in the Medway attacked Chatham and Sheerness, sailing away with the *Royal Charles* the English flagship in tow. The populace and Parliament desperate for a scapegoat rounded on Clarendon who was impeached and sent into exile. It had not escaped the notice of some that the Dutch were Calvinists as were the persecuted English nonconformists, who were insisting that God had a controversy with the nation. By now the irreligious Charles II was weary of posing as the champion of the Church of England and possibly already had secret yearnings in the direction of Roman Catholicism. Parliament however was in no mood to ease the lot of the nonconformists, although in practice things became easier for a time especially in the London area. In December 1667, Samuel Pepys noted, 'The Nonconformists are mighty high and their meetings frequented and connived at; and they do expect to have their day now soon; for my Lord Buckingham [a member of the King's inner council] is a declared friend of them and even of the Quakers.'[22]

By this time Owen appears as the pastor of an Independent church in London. This may well have been the church he formed in 1659. The membership does not appear to have been large but included a number of former leaders of the Commonwealth and their families.

By 1668 it was evident that fines and imprisonments had not wiped out nonconformity. Another attempt was made to modify the settlement. Nonconformist leaders were approached. John Wilkins bishop of Chester was willing to promote a fresh plan to incorporate the Presbyterians within the Church Of England. Richard Baxter and Thomas Manton were pleased to enter into negotiations. Owen hoped that at the same time orthodox Independents could be given toleration outside the Church of England if they accepted the doctrinal articles of the Established Church. Buckingham was willing to promote this. The House of Commons was furious when it discovered what was afoot and refused to consider either suggestion. Manton was displeased with Owen, considering that talk of toleration had wrecked the whole plan. Other Presbyterians including Samuel Annesley saw that comprehension was unrealistic and that it would be wiser for Nonconformists to form a united front to press for toleration. Baxter was hurt by the failure of the comprehension plan. A few months later Owen was promoting plans for Independent and Presbyterian co-operation in the face of persecution. Baxter accepted the idea, but recorded that he sternly warned Owen,

> that I must deal freely with him; that when I thought of what he had done formerly, I was much afraid lest one that had been so great a breaker, would not be made an instrument of healing. But in other respects I thought him the fittest man in England for this work; partly because he could understand the case, and partly because his experience of the humours of men, and of the mischiefs of dividing principles and practices had been so very great, that if experience should make any man wise and fit for a healing work it should be him.

The discussions broke down because Baxter saw union as a step towards comprehension in the Church of England, whereas

Owen wanted it to be a means of achieving toleration for Dissenters outside the Church of England. Owen also considered that a more detailed doctrinal statement was necessary than did Baxter.[23]

Meanwhile there were threats of greater persecution. In 1670 Parliament passed the First Test Act which increased the penalties for nonconformity. Owen protested in vain. In the meantime Charles II had signed the secret Treaty of Dover promising Louis XIV of France that in due time he would declare himself a Roman Catholic. He needed to alleviate the lot of the Roman Catholics. He could not do this without helping the Nonconformists. The upshot was a Declaration of Indulgence, allowing Roman Catholics to worship in their own homes and granting Nonconformists toleration as long as they obtained licences for their meeting places and for their ministers. Owen was involved in discussions with government officials before this arrangement was made. It should be emphasised that there is no evidence that he was aware of the ignominious conditions of the Secret Treaty of Dover, which was unknown even to many of the king's ministers. Owen's views on the Church of Rome were clear. He continued to warn against it in writing and from the pulpit until the end of his life. As far as the practical outworking of the Indulgence went Owen was active in helping his fellow ministers to obtain licences although there is no evidence that he ever had one himself. The Declaration of Indulgence led to a great spate of Nonconformist activity, but the Indulgence itself lasted only for one year. Parliamentary pressure compelled the king to withdraw it.

The 1670s were years of activity by the Nonconformists in spite of the fact that their worship was strictly illegal and sporadic persecution continued through the country. Owen was often consulted by his brethren and did what he could to help them. On one occasion the king gave him a thousand guineas to relieve suffering Nonconformists. One whom Owen highly esteemed was John Bunyan. He found a publisher for *The Pilgrim's Progress*, sending Bunyan to his own publisher, Nathaniel Ponder. Charles II once asked Owen why such a cultured man as himself listened to the preaching of a tinker. Owen's reply was, 'I would gladly exchange my learning for the ability of that tinker to touch men's hearts.'

In 1673 Joseph Caryl died. His church called John Owen to succeed him. Owen's church was smaller and the two churches merged, meeting in Leadenhall Street in the City. Owen continued as pastor of this church until his death ten years later. These years were times of tremendous energy. In addition the demands on his leadership abilities, and pastoral and preaching responsibilities, Owen was writing extensively. I have referred to the output of controversial material. His massive work on the epistle to the Hebrews appeared in four folio volumes between 1668 and 1684. His *Discourse on the Holy Spirit* appeared in 1674. Further related pieces on the Holy Spirit were written in the remaining years. Other works include *Apostasy* 1676, *Justification by Faith* 1677, *The Person of Christ* 1678, *The Grace and Duty of being Spiritually-minded,* 1681 and the incomparable, *Meditations and Discourses on the Glory of Christ* which did not appear until the year after his death. These are but a selection from the output of these years. One is not surprised to discover that he had assistants during these years, the best known of whom was David Clarkson who was serving the church at the time of Owen's death.

Mary Owen, John's first wife died in January 1676. She was a devoted wife. They had several children, but sadly most died in early life. After eighteen months Owen married again, this time Dorothy, the widow of Thomas D'Oyley, a member of the landlords' family at Stadhampton. She was a wealthy woman and Owen himself had received a substantial legacy some time before. Although his health was giving cause for concern in the late 1670s, he was able to live in greater comfort, even keeping a horse and carriage, causing some hostile comment. He suffered increasingly from asthma and internal disorders and moved to Ealing, then a village outside London. From there he continued to travel to his church in the City. These last years took their toll. Andrew Thomson records, 'He is said to have stooped considerably during the latter years of his life', contrasting this with reports that 'when in full vigour his person was tall and majestic'.[24]

As Owen weakened physically the dark clouds of persecution were again threatening. Charles II's political opponents had been able to give him a hard time in the late 1670s. They tried to exclude his brother, James Duke of York from the succession because of his Romanism. Their methods had been unscrupulous, but in 1682 the king struck back at his foes undermining their power base in the corporation of the City of London. As the reaction gathered momentum so the authorities turned against the Nonconformists whom they suspected of being secret republicans. In the face of the threatening political storm Owen dictated his last surviving letter, to his old friend, Charles Fleetwood on 22nd August 1683.

> I am going to him whom my soul hath loved, or rather hath loved me with an everlasting love; which is the whole ground of all my consolation. The passage is very irksome and wearisome through strong pain of various sorts which are all issued in an intermitting fever. All things were provided to carry me to London today attending to the advice of my physician, but we were all disappointed by my utter disability to undertake the journey. I am leaving the ship of the church in a storm, but while the great Pilot is in it the loss of a poore under-rower will be inconsiderable. Live and pray and hope and waite patiently and doe not despair; the promise stands invincible that he will never leave thee nor forsake thee.[25]

Two days later he had a visit from his friend William Payne who was supervising the printing of *The Glory of Christ*. Payne assured him that the work was proceeding well. Owen replied, 'I am glad to hear it; but O brother Payne! The long wished-for day is come at last, in which I shall see the glory in another manner than I have ever done, or was capable of doing in this world.' Later that day the end came. It was the 24th August 1683, St Bartholomew's Day, exactly twenty one years after the Great Ejection which had driven Puritanism into the wilderness. Over five more years were to pass before at long last the Dissenting Churches were granted toleration.

On 4th September John Owen was buried in Bunhill Fields where the bodies of so many of his associates lay. The great crowd at his funeral included nobility as well as a vast host of humble people who had loved and respected this faithful teacher who had guided them and stood by them in the bitter years of persecution.

How should we assess this man of many talents, in turn a country pastor, an army chaplain, head of an Oxford college, vice chancellor before becoming a leader among the persecuted Nonconformists? I leave an assessment of his theology to later speakers. I suspect that Owen, like so many of his Puritan brothers, saw his real calling to be that of a pastor. In those early days at Fordham he had always described himself thus, rather than using the traditional term, 'parson'. As a pastor Owen had always laid great emphasis on preaching. It was his preaching that had attracted the attention of the grandees of the Commonwealth. That preaching was concerned above all with the glory of God in Christ and the spiritual welfare of his people. He was the man who pleaded for the provision of gospel preaching throughout the land with special concern for the needs of Wales and Ireland. Unlike the political Nonconformists of the late nineteenth and early twentieth centuries there is no evidence that he wished to be involved in the minutiae of politics. Baxter claimed that at times he went too far in political involvement. This may be true, but I would suggest that those times were few and must be seen as an aside from his main business.

Biographers have complained of the difficulty of getting close to this stately figure who moved easily among politicians and dons. Certainly his diaries are lost and there is a paucity of personal detail. His letters at times reveal a dry humour, but I suggest that you can get to him, by reading his sermons. There you see something of the exercises of his soul and then turn to *The Glory of Christ* to see how this remarkable man prepared himself to die.

Notes

[1] John Owen, *The Works of John Owen, D.D.*, edited by William Goold, Edinburgh, 1862, vol. 13, p.224.

[2] *Works,* 10, p.147.

[3] W*orks,* 8, p.170,1.

[4] *Works,* 8, p. 165.

[5] *Works,* 8. p. 276

[6] John Asty quoted, Andrew Thomson, 'Life of Dr Owen', *Works,* 1, p.xlii.

[7] *Works,* 10, p. 479.

[8] *Works,* 8, pp, 235,6.

[9] *Works,* 10, p. 402.

[10] Peter Toon, *God's Statesman: The Life and Work of John Owen,* Exeter (Paternoster Press), 1971, p.51.

[11] *The Oxford Orations of Dr John Owen,* ed. Peter Toon, Callington, Cornwall, n.d., p.45.

[12] Quoted, Peter Toon, *God's Statesman,* Exeter, 1971, p. 79.

[13] John Owen, *Biblical Theology,* trans. Stephen Westcott, Soli Deo Gloria, 1994.

[14] Quoted, Toon, *God's Statesman,* p. 55.

[15] Richard Baxter, *Autobiography,* Everyman's Library, 1931, p.70.

[16] Williston Walker, *The Creeds and Platforms of Congregationalism,* Boston, USA, 1960 [1893], 'The Savoy Declaration Preface', p. 359.

[17] Quoted, Andrew Thomson, 'Life of Dr Owen', *Works,* 1, p. lxx.

[18] *Works,* 8, p.467.

[19] Quoted Toon, *God's Statesman,* p. 113.

[20] *Works,* 15, p.24.

[21] *Works,* 15, p.33.

[22] Quoted , Toon, *God's Statesman,* p. 133

[23] See Toon, *God's Statesman* pp. 135,6 for a fuller discussion of these events.

[24] *Works,* 1, p. civ.

[25] Peter Toon, *The Correspondence of John Owen,* Cambridge, 1970, p. 174.

Chapter Two

JOHN OWEN AS A THEOLOGIAN

Carl Trueman has lectured in Church
History and Historical Theology in the
Universities of Nottingham and
Aberdeen. He is currently Associate
Professor of Church History and
Historical Theology at Westminster
Theological Seminary Philadelphia.
He is the author of *Luther's Legacy:
Salvation and the English Reformers*
and *The Claims of Truth: John Owen's
Trinitarian Theology*

Whatever the Son of God wrought in, by, or upon the human nature, he did it by the Holy Spirit, as he is the Spirit of the Father.

Works 3, p. 162

JOHN OWEN AS A THEOLOGIAN

Introduction

It is a somewhat daunting task to be asked to give a lecture of approximately one-hour on the topic of John Owen as theologian. Some years ago I had the pleasure of examining a PhD thesis with John Webster, Professor of Divinity in the University of Oxford and whose chair is attached to Christ Church, Owen's old college. When he saw the set of Owen's works on my shelves, he turned to me and commented that he considered the Puritan to be the finest theological mind that England ever had produced. Admittedly, the competition is not great, since England has generally been home to great biblical scholars rather than theologians, but still praise indeed – and an indication that my subject today is far higher, wider and deeper than I can possibly convey within the limitations of a single chapter.

Given these limitations, I want to make three basic points about Owen as theologian which will serve to set his work within the Western theological tradition as a whole. As a result, there will be many obvious facets of Owen's theology which receive no treatment at all in this chapter. I would stress therefore at the outset that my choice of topics is not intended as any kind of absolute value judgement but simply the result of the need to keep within appropriate limits. Given this, the three points I would wish to make are as follows: first, Owen was an extremely

well-educated and learned theologian; second, he was a vigorously anti-Pelagian theologian; and, third, he was a firmly
Trinitarian theologian. The three points are, in a sense, all varia-
tions on a single theme. My contention is that Owen's theology
was overwhelmingly shaped by his doctrine of God, and its
counterpoint in his understanding of humanity, and that these
were not 'Owen's' doctrines as such; rather, Owen's
articulation of these doctrines was dependent upon the catholic
theology of the historic Western church as a whole. Furthermore, I do not wish to make a simple leap from the seventeenth century to the present day and argue that all Owen had
to say is directly applicable to us in its original shape and form;
but I do wish to commend Owen to students, ministers, and
thoughtful Christians in general, as a good example of how
theology can be done in a serious and profound manner.

I. Owen as a Learned Theologian

We need to be clear at the start that Owen's breadth of learning
was much broader than his description as a 'Puritan' might
initially lead us to believe. Too often today 'Puritanism' carries
ascetic, obscurantist, sectarian connotations which are not
appropriate when applied to thinkers such as Owen, and we do
well to rid ourselves of them at the outset. He was, after all, a
highly educated individual, trained at the University of Oxford
and thoroughly versed in historic intellectual culture of Western
Europe. As a result, his mind was profoundly shaped by the
intellectual currents which were flowing through the university in
the seventeenth century and which had been shaped by centuries of scholarly endeavour.[1] We must at the outset rid
ourselves of any idea that Owen's intellectual tradition started
in the early sixteenth century, something which seems to be a
constant temptation for those who look back to the Reformation

for their theological roots. The curriculum he would have studied, while developing rapidly and subject to powerful forces from the Renaissance, exhibited many points of continuity with the medieval course of study which stretched back to the twelfth century. The libraries to which he would have had access would have contained large numbers of medieval tomes. The logic which he would have been taught was essentially continuous with what had been taught in the Middle Ages. The metaphysics to which he would have been exposed had its basic agenda set by the various debates that had erupted in the medieval period between the differing philosophical schools within the church, supremely the debates which went on over the nature of being between the respective followers of Thomas Aquinas, John Duns Scotus and William of Occam. Owen's mind, then would have been filled with the kind of questions and answers which the medieval schoolmen raised in their classroom debates and, as I have argued elsewhere, what we have in Owen's theology as a philosophical level is a modified version of the thought of Thomas Aquinas.[2] This is not of course, to say that Owen's overall theology is essentially compatible at all points with that of Thomas and the Thomistic traditions which took their cue from his writings; but is to make clear that we should not be tricked by the anti-medieval rhetoric we find throughout Puritan works into believing that they did not borrow heavily from their medieval predecessors. As university trained men of learning, they could not really do otherwise. Thus, when Owen died, his library catalogue was full of books of medieval scholasticism and Renaissance Jesuit philosophy, and even a cursory glance at his writings reveals how much he owed to these authors.[3] He knew good and clever arguments when he met them, as he did frequently in his university education and subsequent reading; and he was not afraid to use them when they suited his purpose.[4]

One reason why Thomas appealed to Owen was almost certainly because he represented part of the Western anti-Pelagian tradition within which Owen located himself and which look back to the work of Augustine for much of its inspiration. This brings us to a further aspect of Owen's work: his patristic learning. The Reformation was fuelled in part by the massive recovery of patristic knowledge which the culture of the Renaissance encouraged and the advent of the printing press made possible. After centuries where the learning of the early church fathers was mediated to the present by books of extracted quotations, or 'sentences', which were arranged thematically but whose meaning was often distorted by lack of context, scholars from the fifteenth century onwards had started to produce critical editions of original patristic works. Beneficiaries of this scholarship included, among others, Martin Luther and John Calvin.[5] Central to this patristic reclamation project were the writings of Augustine and, while the sixteenth century was marked by a deepening knowledge of a wide range of Fathers, the central patristic debates of the Reformation focused on the interpretation of Augustine and to what extent he could be claimed as fully Protestant or fully Catholic. The problem, of course, was that he was fully neither, being a far more ambiguous figure than either Protestants or Catholics acknowledged. Indeed B. B. Warfield's claim that the Reformation represented the triumph of Augustine's doctrine of grace over his doctrine of the church is a judgement with more than a grain of truth.[6]

As we might expect from one of the foremost men of intellectual culture of his day, Owen was himself part of this rebirth of first-hand patristic knowledge. His library catalogue revealed extensive holdings in all the major Fathers, Latin and Greek. In addition, his love of Augustine is evident throughout his writings. To document this exhaustively would take an excessive amount of time and prove somewhat fruitless; and certainly the subsequent discussions in this paper of his anti-Pelagianism and Trinitarianism will inevitably point to his profound debts to Augustine in an unequivocal manner in both his doctrines of God, creation, and salvation. The impact of Augustine on Owen was pervasive, exemplified perhaps by his use of Augustine's masterpiece, *The Confessions,* as the classic description and normative pattern of Christian experience. The influence of this work on the general Western Christian tradition is well-known, where it was made, in the words of Jaroslav Pelikan into a 'a paradigm of the inner life'.[7] This was most certainly true for Owen who assigned the work a central paradigmatic role in his own *magnum opus* on the work of the Holy Spirit.[8]

From the above, it is clear that Owen's thinking was truly catholic in the best sense of being both learned and wide-ranging in its relation to the broader theological tradition. Owen was, however above all a Protestant and this leads us to the central inte-grating point of his intellectual life: the importance of scripture. It is, of course, hardly surprising that Owen, as a Reformed Protestant, assigned scripture a central role; yet even here we should take care to note the connection between his commit-ment to the scripture principle and his commitment to learning and careful scholarship, a point reflected in his attitude to the biblical languages. From its very inception at the hands of Martin Luther, Protestant education had placed knowledge of the biblical languages at the very heart of its theological and minis-terial training. This was for the very simple reason that Protes-tantism, with its high view of the unique nature and authority of the biblical canon, inevitably demanded that its leaders be acquainted with the texts of that canon in their original languages. To have failed in this area would thus have made a practical nonsense of the theological commitment to the scrip-tural authority. Owen himself gives four reasons why know-ledge of the languages is to be desired among those who seek to lead the church: divine inspiration refers to the original texts, not translations; every jot, tittle and subtlety of the original is therefore of great importance; the emphases and texture of the originals are lost or obscured in translation; and the idiomatic nature of scriptural language requires broad familiarity with cognate literature in the original languages.[9] In other words, the minister or theologian should ideally not have just grasped the rudiments of Hebrew and Greek but should also have a profound understanding of the languages and the cultures from which they arose. To put it bluntly, Protestant commitment to the notion of *sola scriptura* required nothing less than the training of ministers in the solid, classical traditions of linguistic excellence.[10]

This last point serves to indicate that Owen's commitment to learning. Being a Renaissance man, familiar with literature, philosophy and culture, was not incidental to his theologising but was in fact an integral part of it, arising directly from his commitment to the notion of a God who had revealed himself in scripture. Scripture is profound; and, if its profoundest points are to be grasped, then the minister must have the learning necessary. This does not, undermine commitment to the essential perspicuity of scripture – Owen famously declared that he would rather have John Bunyan's gifts as a preacher than all his learning – but it does acknowledge that the task of biblical exegesis at its highest level requires considerable learning and intellectual cultivation. It is no coincidence that the British Puritans, like their Dutch counterparts, were on the whole learned, educated men for whom a high level of intellectual and scholarly accomplishment was something which should normally precede any kind of fruitful Christian leadership or ministry. They were, we might say, Reformed in the truest sense of the word: not simply committed to the so-called 'five points of Calvinism' but also committed to a way of doing theology which was articulate and which took account of the broad contours of theological tradition and which prided itself on its education and acumen. This, I would suggest, is something of importance for today when we reflect upon what theological education is meant to be. When looking back at the Puritans through the lens of later evangelical revivalism, there is a tendency either to downplay their learning as incidental to their ministry or to allow divisions in the ecclesiastical sphere to narrow the content of the theological curriculum to those authors of whom we approve. This was not the Reformation way: it is beyond dispute that the Reformation arose in large part as an intellectual movement through the reforming of university theological curricula, and that its success lay on one level in the effectiveness with which it wrought the necessary changes; and, if anti-intellectualism was not the Reformation way, neither was it the Puritan way. Indeed, their learning was essential to their project: they needed the languages and the literary skills precisely because they held to a high view of scripture and they read the works of their opponents because they knew that polemics had to be conducted from a position of knowledge if they were to be any use, and that the historical tradition of Christianity, while containing much rubbish, also contained a great store of wisdom.[11] Owen appears to have regarded a good argument, as sound concept, or a useful set of terms to be fair game no matter what its origins or who its author.[12]

I want to close this section by giving just one example of how this learning was deployed by Owen to strengthen his theology. As a good Reformed theologian, Owen regarded God as self-existent, sovereign and transcendent. This meant, among other things, that the very possibility of theology, of human speech about God, depended upon God's initiative. To put it bluntly, men and women could only talk about God once God himself had spoken and given them words to say. Now, Owen regarded God's own knowledge of himself in its very nature as perfect, eternal and infinite. It was therefore something which by its very nature could belong to God alone because humanity, even pre-Fall humanity, through its very finitude, could never possess such knowledge of God; therefore' human theology depended entirely upon the divine initiative. It was therefore necessary that God reveal himself and that he do so in a way suited to human finitude. To express this in clear and precise terms, Owen used the classic medieval terminology of archetype and ectype to refer respectively to these divine and human theologies.[13] This pair of terms had their origin in the Middle Ages, and had been brought into use in Protestant circles by the Reformed theologian, Francis Junius.[14] What they did was allow for the concise expression of a theological concept which lay at the very heart of Owen's anti-Pelagian theology. God's knowledge of himself was infinite and this was known as archetypal theology. It was inaccessible to human knowledge. God's revelation of himself, accommodated to human finitude and revealed within created time and space, was ectypal: that is, it was true, but limited to human capacity and thus not an exhaustive revelation of who God was.

The terminology therefore allowed Owen to delineate the relationship between God in himself and God as he has revealed himself to humanity in a way which did justice to God's infinity and unknowableness, and yet which also emphasised the basic truthfulness and reliability of his revelation. The point was crucial to a defence of the orthodox understanding of God against a mysticism which sought to deny humanity any positive knowledge of God and a rationalism which sought to posit an identity between the limits of humanity's knowledge and limits of God himself. Yet clear expression of the idea depended upon Reformed Orthodoxy's grasp of the language and concepts of the Medieval theological tradition. Indeed, Owen reinforced this with further terms borrowed from that same tradition: in addition to describing human theology as ectypal, he also characterised it using the medieval Latin terms *viator* ('traveller') and *possessor* ('possessor') to distinguish between the knowledge of God which believers have by faith during their earthly pilgrimage and that which the saints have by sight in heaven.[15] These sets of technical terms express Owen 's commitment to safeguarding the divine initiative in revelation and thus in theology; they also demonstrate his wide learning and his debt to the concepts and language of medieval thought, and the way in which like Reformed Orthodox contemporaries, he was able to enlist these for the defence and propagation of the Reformed faith. This is just one example, but it is typical of his eclectic attitude to the earlier theological tradition with which he obviously had a profound acquaintance.

II. Owen as Anti-Pelagian Theologian

Owen's learning, of course, found expression in his many theological writings and these writings were themselves shaped by the polemical concern which dominated his life. While he was at the centre of numerous controversies during his lifetime, he was preoccupied more than anything else with two schools of heretical theology: Arminianism and Socinianism. The two should, of course, be distinguished. Arminianism was, in its most orthodox expression, Trinitarian and, in a broad sense, part of the tradition of classical theism;[16] while Socinianism had at its very heart a firm rejection of the traditional understanding of the triunity of God. Instead Socinians argued for a unitarian conception whereby only the Father is the true self-existent and eternal divinity.[17] Nevertheless the boundary between the two was somewhat fluid, as the debates surrounding the appointment of Vorstius at the University of Leiden indicate. Certainly in the minds of the Reformed Orthodox, Socinianism was regarded as the outcome of a consistent Arminianism.[18]

From the very inception of his publishing career with *A Display of Arminianism* in 1642, combating Arminian and Socinian ideas was a constant refrain of his writings.[19] Some of his work (especially of the earlier period) attacks straw men, particularly in his tendency to deal with his opponents in terms of the extreme logical implications of their thought rather than what they actually said.[20] Nevertheless, two issues stand at the heart of Owen's thinking at this point which must be central to any understanding of him as a theologian: a belief in the sovereignty of God and an understanding of the radical nature of human sinfulness and evil. For Owen, the Arminian notion of free will is obnoxious precisely because it serves to delimit God's sovereignty and lessen the nature of human sinfulness. To put it in modern terms, it sentimentalised both God and human nature, and that is why Arminianism was to Owen one of the most dangerous schools of thought within the church. This is summarised in the two motivations which Owen argues underlie the Arminian theology. Arminians, he says, strive '[t]o exempt themselves from God's jurisdiction, to free themselves from the supreme dominion of his all-ruling providence' and 'to clear human nature from the heavy imputation of being sinful, corrupted, wise to do evil but unable to do good'.[21] Under these two heads, Owen lists the various ways in which these basic motivations work themselves out in reconstruction of the divine decrees, of original sin and of Christ's death on the cross. Thus, we see that the debate about Arminianism, while superficially concerned with providence and sin, has profound implications for Trinitarian and christological doctrine as well. This is not for Owen a battle which merely relates to alternative views of predestination but which strikes deep at the doctrine of God and thus at the doctrines of everything else.[22]

The doctrines of sovereignty and sin are themselves intimately related. In his massive Latin work of 1661, *Theologoumena Pantodapa,* Owen chose to structure his discussion of theology around the framework of the biblical covenants, specifically those with Adam, Noah, Abraham and Moses, culminating in the advent of Christ.[23] The choice of such a structure is significant. First, it indicates Owen's position within the larger tradition of Protestant theologians who chose the biblical covenants as a means of structuring their theological discussion. Second, it represents an attempt to articulate a theology which set a comprehensive scheme for the interpretation of biblical history at its very centre. Both of these points are important to any contextualised understanding of Owen as a theologian and deserve exploration of a kind that is not possible here. There is, however, a third point: it reflects Owen's belief that all theology is relational in that it involves God revealing himself to humanity in a manner that is all-determinative of the relationship that then exists between the two. This kind of theology cannot be reduced to a collection of abstract, unrelated and uncoordinated doctrines; rather, the doctrines themselves all cast light upon the relationship that exists between God and humanity. Thus, knowledge of God and knowledge of self are, in Calvin's famous phrase, 'joined by many bonds'. As a result, Christian doctrine is both self-involving as it relates intimately to the status of the knower in terms of the known; and, furthermore, one cannot tinker with the one doctrine without tinkering with the others since they are all part of one larger whole. Thus, the statement that humanity is sinful has implications for understanding the nature of God and the statement God is sovereign has implications for understanding the nature of sinful men and women.

It would take far too long to explore in this paper all the points of antithesis between Reformed Orthodoxy and Arminianism on the interrelated doctrines of God and humanity, so I will restrict myself to two points: first, the different understanding of God's sovereignty and, second, the different understandings of Christ's work which are rooted in differing understanding of humanity's sin. The connection between the first and second points should be obvious to all but the least theologically sensitive.

First, grace. Of course, grace cannot be discussed for Owen in isolation from the large question of the relation of God's will to the created realm, and here Owen's discussion follows a path familiar to the Western anti-Pelagian tradition. By arguing that God can will something which does not come to pass, Owen claims that Arminians inevitably argue that grace is resistible. The issue with the Arminians is in one important dimension a question of exegesis. The Arminiams, according to Owen, fail to realise that scriptural expressions about the will of God need to be distinguished in order to avoid having scripture plainly contradict itself, as in the case of Abraham being told by God to sacrifice Isaac despite scriptural strictures on murder and sacrifice.[24] The problem is that the Arminians fail to realise that the divine will, which is simple and non-contradictory, is yet diverse in its revelation. What is superficially an exegetical dispute in fact finds its roots in utterly different conceptions of God.[25]

Second, Owen draws on the vocabulary and concepts of the medieval tradition. He argues that scriptural statements about humanity's duty towards God should not be confused with God's actual will about what shall come to pass. Owen describes the former category of statements as God's 'will of the sign' or God's revealed will, and the latter as God's secret or hidden will. Distinctions of this kind are commonplace in western theology from Augustine onwards, though Owen is happy to acknowledge his personal debt to Aquinas on this score.[26] This distinction is necessary for the whole notion of human autonomy regarding the will – a position demanded even by the Arminian notion of middle knowledge – would give human beings an ontological status similar to that of God and thus theologically unacceptable because it would fail to do justice to scriptural teaching about God as the only self-existent, self sufficient and autonomous being.[27]

This group of metaphysical arguments is, of course, not deployed in the interest of creating an independent philosophical doctrine of God but in order to make the various texts of scripture cohere with each other. Following on from this, it is clear that the whole question of God's will in general has specific implications for the question of grace in particular. If God's will could be resisted, then his grace could be resisted; and, if that is so, the theologian has to ask if it is even hypothetically possible that such grace would not be resisted. For Owen, as for other Reformed theologians, this must be denied: humanity's sinful state means that they are at enmity with God and will not turn to him even if grace is offered.

In *A Display of Arminianism,* Owen discusses human potential for choosing to accept God's grace; first, providing a massive list of scriptural texts which speak of human depravity and inability for the good.[28] This is then followed by a theological argument in three parts, asserting the need for supernatural power to achieve a supernatural result.[29] Finally, he cites as further support both the articles of the Church of England (of which, of course, he was a serving minister) and more scripture passages.[30] Owen's position on this issue was not to undergo any substantial change during his career, and yet we must remember that the work in which these arguments appear was his first attempt at polemical theology.

Years later, in his massive treatise on the work of the Holy Spirit, Owen returns to the theme. Here, while we see the old refrain of natural human impotency reprised, we also see the deepening sophistication of Owen's own theology as he set the whole argument with an explicitly Trinitarian framework. Having discussed the radical nature of human moral impotence, he outlines the origin and nature of spiritual life:

The fountain of this life being in God and fullness of it
being laid up in Christ for us, he communicates the
power and principle of it unto us by the Holy Ghost ...
The spiritual life is communicated unto us by the Holy
Ghost, according unto and in order for the ends of the
new covenant: for this is the promise of it, That God will
first write his law in our hearts, and then we shall walk
in his statutes; that is, the principle of life and precede
all vital acts ... The same thing is intended when we say
in other words, that without an infused habit of internal
inherent grace, received from Christ by an efficacious
work of the Spirit, no man can believe or obey God, or
perform any duty in a saving manner, so as it should be
accepted with him.[31]

Though the thought here is consistent with his earlier teaching
on the subject, the Trinitarian note is sounded with much more
vigour, indicating that we are here witnessing the mature and
sophisticated reflections of Owen on the nature of human
salvation as it is rooted in the Trinitarian economy of grace.
Divine sovereignty and human moral impotence demand a
Trinitarian response on the part of the Trinitarian God, and that
is what Owen is here articulating. Thus we see how the issue of
an anti-Pelagian theology involves not simply bald questions
about the metaphysics of the Creator-creature relationship, but
also pushes Owen back to reflecting upon the Trinitarian nature
and acts of God himself. It is not surprising, there for, that the
battle with Arminianism over grace was regarded as closely
related to the battle with Socinianism over the Trinitarian
nature of God.

A further element of the anti-Pelagian dimension of Owen's
theology relates to his christology, and again we can here trace
both consistency and development within his thinking on this
issue. In the first chapter of A *Display of Arminianism,* Owen
claims that one result of the Arminian modification of the
doctrine of human sinfulness is a revision of the work of Christ:

> They deny the efficacy of the merit of the death of Christ;
> both that God intended by his death to redeem his church
> or to acquire himself a holy people; as also, that Christ,
> by his death, hath merited and procured us grace, faith
> or righteousness, and power to obey God, in fulfilling
> the condition of the new covenant[32]

The issue of Christ's work in Owen's theology is a highly complex one which I have dealt with in more detail elsewhere, but a few comments here are in order. First, we must not be misled by the anachronistic term 'limited atonement' into thinking that the point at issue is that of the so-called extent of the atonement, i.e., whether Christ died for everyone or only for some. Such a naïve way of posing the question issue simply begs more questions. The real point at issue is whether Christ's blood is efficacious for salvation, i.e., whether it is part of one, seamless economy of salvation which leads to the salvation of those individuals whom God has elected to eternal life. As such, the question primarily stands in positive relation to the issues of Christ's mediation and of his priestly office rather than the more speculative questions concerning the alleged logic of decretal theology.

Second, we must once again realise that Owen's thinking on this issue develops over time, while yet retaining central motifs. In *A Display of Arminianism*, for example, Owen is quite clear that the death of Christ cannot be isolated from his continued oblation of himself through his heavenly intercession:

> His intercession in heaven is nothing but a continued
> oblation of himself. So that whatsoever Christ
> impetrated, merited, or obtained by his death and
> passion must be infallibly applied unto and bestowed
> upon them for whom he intended to obtain it; or else
> his intercession is vain, he is not heard in the prayers of
> his mediatorship .... We must not so disjoin the offices

of Christ's mediatorship, that one of them may be versated about some towards whom he exerciseth not the other; much less ought we so to separate the several acts of the same office. [33]

This focus on the priesthood of Christ as the controlling context for understanding the work of Christ in salvation is of crucial importance to Owen's thinking throughout his career. It is certainly true that his opinion on at least one issue relating to Christ's work changed radically over time. In *A Display of Arminianism* he argues that Christ's death for sin was only necessary because God willed it to be so; later he argues that, if God was ever to forgive sin then the death of Christ was absolutely necessary.[34] Nevertheless, the focus on mediation and priesthood remained a constant refrain and, like the discussion of grace, was developed and enriched within the context of Trinitarian discussions.

A good example of this is provided by the classic work, *The Death of Death,* where the framework of the treatise as laid out in Book One is explicitly Trinitarian, ascribing differing acts to Father, Son and Holy Spirit, with the typical Augustinian caveat that all external acts of the Trinity are to be understood as involving all three persons.[35] The argument of the treatise as a whole is then rooted in the Trinitarian economy outlined at the start: God the Father commissions the Son as Mediator; the Son accepts the role as Mediator and executes; and the Holy Spirit through effecting the incarnation, Christ's death and his resurrection, brings the work to completion[36] In this scheme we see the working out of the implications of Christ's actions as substitute for sinners in relation to the doctrine of the trinity, an advance in sophistication, though not in basic concern, from the treatise of 1642. Indeed, controversy with Baxter on this issue then led to further sharpening of the Trinitarian context of Christ's mediatorship, with Owen arguing that discussion of the

merit of Christ's death outside of the context of his appointment as mediator (and thus outside of the Trinitarian framework of salvation) is meaningless as it is this very framework
which constitutes Christ's death as an offering for sin.[37]

As with the discussion of grace and sin, it is clear from this
that Owen's discussion of christology within the anti-Pelagian
framework of salvation, points towards the Trinitarian foundations of his thinking. I indicated earlier that I believed his thought
could be characterised as an extended reflection on the mutual
implications of anti-Pelagian notions of grace and sin, and of
Trinitarianism. Here is evidence that such a claim is essentially
correct. Starting with sin, with grace, or with Christ, Owen's
thought is led again and again to probe the Trinitarian foundations of Christian theology, and this leads to my third basic
point: that Owen was not just a learned theologian, nor an
anti-Pelagian theologian, but also a Trinitarian theologian.

III. Owen as Trinitarian Theologian

It is impossible to do justice to the richness of Owen's
Trinitarianism in a single paper, and so I intend to highlight
simply one or two aspects of his thinking in this area in this final
and much briefer section.

First, Owen's Trinitarianism is thoroughly catholic. He is
entirely comfortable with the traditional language of substance
and persons, and holds explicitly to the classic idea that all
external acts of God involve all three persons of the Godhead.[38]
He also maintains the specifically Western order of the procession of the Persons, whereby the Son is eternally generated by
the Father, and the Spirit proceeds from both the Father *and*
the Son. In this area, Owen simply adopts the established tradition wholesale, as one would expect.[39]

Second, the Trinity lies at the heart of Owen's understanding of the economy of salvation in both its eternal foundation and its historical outworking. If all external acts of God are necessary Trinitarian, then salvation itself has to have a Trinitarian basis. Owen, along with his Reformed contemporaries, spent much time reflecting on the implications of God's saving action in time for his activity in eternity. In eternity, Owen sees the plan of salvation as established in agreement between Father, Son and Holy Spirit to accomplish redemption in time. This he refers to as the covenant of redemption, and describes it as follows: the Father agrees to send the Son and to establish him as Mediator between God and humanity; the Son, consubstantial with the Father, agrees voluntarily to the arrangement and submits himself to the Father's will; and the Holy Spirit accepts the task both of forging salvation within time by being the agent who both communicates the properties of divine nature to the human nature of Christ and who applies the benefits of Christ's death to the elect. Then, in time, this whole economy is executed through the agency of the Holy Spirit.[40]

Much could be said about this aspect of Owen's thought. For example, it serves to preserve the consubstantiality of the persons while yet explaining their economic differences and, in the case of the Son, his functional subordination to the Father. Most interesting, however, one area which will repay further reflection is the role of Spirit. Owen's pneumatology is profound. Building on the Western tradition with its emphasis on the *filioque,* all his discussion of the Spirit has a profound Christ-focus because the Spirit proceeds from both Father and Son. Thus, when the Spirit acts, he acts always in relation to the Son. To say, therefore, that Owen is a theologian of the Holy Spirit is at the same time to say that Owen is a theologian of the Christ. As he himself declares:

> The Holy Spirit is the Spirit of the Son, no less than the Spirit of the Father. He proceedeth from the Son, as from the Father ... And hence is he the immediate operator of all divine acts of the Son himself, even on his own human nature. Whatever the Son of God wrought in, by, or upon the human nature, he did it by the Holy Ghost, who is his Spirit, as he is the Spirit of the Father.[41]

These are deep theological waters but the essential point is clear: the Son does not work without the Spirit; and the Spirit does not work without the Son. The principle that all external acts of the Godhead involve all three persons of the Trinity holds good even in the actions of the Lord Jesus Christ, which stand at the very centre of Christian salvation. The Spirit, therefore, cannot by implication move independently of Christ. In addition, this Spirit-Christology, locates the communication of properties not in the fact of the incarnation itself but in the Spirit's work within the context of the incarnation. This allows Owen to overcome, among other things, the classic problem of Christ's growth in knowledge during his time on earth and thus to underscore his real humanity in a significant manner.[42] Further, the wider implications for theology of this doctrinal point are obvious and dramatic. In terms of both the eternal relations and historic outworking, salvation for Owen does not focus on one person of the Trinity at the expense of the others but involves all; and that is something to which any theology which claims to be distinctively Christian should aspire.

Conclusion

In drawing these brief thoughts on Owen as theologian to a conclusion, I want to make three observations which will bring into sharp relief the differences between the thinking of the great Puritan and much of what passes for Reformed theology in the United Kingdom today.

First, it is quite clear that theological education within the conservative Reformed stream has today lost much of the vision for all-round learning that drove the Reformers and the Reformed Orthodox to shape their theological studies and stock their theological libraries in the way they did. We are uneasy today with the union between learning and piety with which the world of the sixteenth and seventeenth centuries was so comfortable. The fragmentation of the theological discipline, compounded by the divorce of practice and belief has left us, even in orthodox circles, with doubts about the non-negotiable relevance of the biblical languages, of systematic theology, and of thoroughgoing acquaintance with the historic Christian tradition. Such doubts would have been unthinkable to Owen and his contemporaries because all of these things would have been regarded as normative for any who professed commitment to the ideals of Protestant Orthodoxy. In addition, the tendency in some circles to read only approved authors, as if we should only ever open the covers of a book with whose contents we already know we agree, would have been bizarre to a man whose library contained all the classic texts of theology from the early church to his own day – from all major branches of Christendom. Indeed, I suspect Owen would have wondered how anyone could ever learn anything if they only read those authors who they knew they would merely confirm their own positions. English non-conformity has traditionally been suspicious of learning, with, it has to be said, some justification. Nevertheless, it must be stressed that faithful ignorance has little claim to the mantle of the Puritanism of John Owen as does unfaithful learning. We must beware, therefore, of seeking to justify the anti-intellectualism of our tradition, by imputing such to Owen, of remaking him, so to speak, in our own image.

The challenge of the life and work of a man like John Owen is not that he is an example of how he was a Christian theologian in spite of his learning, but rather how he was a Christian theologian precisely through his learning.

Second, Owen's theology is a salutary reminder that we should not allow the current decline in church attendance and status to turn a blind eye in our evangelical ecumenism to the real problems that exist with the evangelical world. I confess here that I am no longer entirely happy being called an evangelical. Where evangelicalism happens to coincide with biblical, historic Christianity, I do not repudiate the description; but in general consider it to be an unhelpful term, if not misleading and meaningless. That it now embraces those who, for example, hold to positions on God's knowledge of the future that are Socinian, it has ceased to be a distinctively Christian term. Owen devoted the greater part of his life to the combatting of Arminianism and its close relative, Socinianism. The ant-Pelagian thrust of Owen's own writings make it quite clear that the differences between Reformed Orthodoxy and classical Arminianism are such that very serious conflicts at a very profound level, exist between the two theologies . This is not to say that classical Arminianism is not 'Christian' in the broadest sense of the work, that it does not preach the Christian gospel in some kind of minimalist way, but it is to say that, beyond that minimum, there are huge areas of disagreement between the Reformed and the Arminian which have implications for everything from divine sovereignty through sin and grace to evangelism and church practice. We should be aware of this and, I would suggest, be a very sceptical of those who always see the threat of faith coming not from the Arminians but from those of a more thoroughly Reformed approach to theology. At a point in history when professed Arminian theologians are beginning once again to espouse positions which, as I have mentioned, are impeccably Socinian in their historical pedigree and would most

certainly be rejected even within the tradition of classical
Arminianism, we need to be aware of where the real lines of
division. I would suggest that the whole thrust of the confes-
sional Reformed tradition, of which Owen's theology is a
superlative example, points towards seeing the differences
between Reformed and Arminians as extremely significant and
momentous. Let us reflect on the implications this has for church
life in the broader sphere.

Finally, we need to reflect once again on the Trinitarian
dimension of the Reformed faith. Historical scholarship has
demonstrated time and again over the last decade that the Trinity
lay at the very heart of Reformed theological thinking, and yet
this is still a note that is largely absent from much Reformed
writing and preaching in the United Kingdom. For Owen, the
doctrine is foundational for understanding creation and salvation, and thus for understanding the very nature not just of
Christian belief but also of practice. We need to make sure that
our faith and practice are distinctively Christian in placing the
Trinitarian God at the centre of our church lives. Further, with
the rising Muslim population in this country, surely there is no
more crucial a time to be reasserting the importance of the
Trinitarian doctrine in our outreach.

Notes

[1] On the culture of Oxford during the lifetime of Owen, see *The History of the University of Oxford, volume IV: Seventeenth Century Oxford*, edited by Nicholas Tyacke (Oxford: Clarendon Press, 1997). On Owen's theology against the background of patristic, medieval and renaissance thought, see Carl R Trueman, *The Claims of Truth: John Owen's Trinitarian Theology* (Carlisle: Paternoster 1998). On Owen's life see Peter Toon, *God's Statesman; the Life and Work of John Owen* (Exeter: Paternoster, 1971); also the opening chapter of Sinclair Ferguson, *John Owen on the Christian Life* (Edinburgh: Banner of Truth, 1987). The Goold edition of Owen's works, published in 24 volumes (London: Johnstone and Hunter, 1850-55) is still the basis source for primary material.

[2] See *The Claims of Truth,* esp. Chapter Three. Further confirmation of this thesis can be found in the arguments of Sebastian Rehnman in 'Theologia Tradita: A Study of the Prolegomenous Discourse of John Owen (1616-1683)', unpublished DPhil dissertation (University of Oxford: 1997)

[3] See for example, his use of the Jesuit Suarez in *A Dissertation on Divine Justice* in *Works* 10.

[4] The posthumous auction catalogue of Owen's library reveals the wide and eclectic nature of his reading. In addition to the standard theological and exegetical works from the patristic era through the Middle Ages to the Reformation, he also had many volumes of classical, medieval, Renaissance and Enlightenment philosophy. A close reading of his own writings reveals his broad familiarity with these categories. In addition to these, fields such as Literature, geography and even beer making were also represented: See *Bibliotheca Oweninana* (London1684)

[5] For studies of the impact of patristic studies on Western theology, including the Reformers, see the essays collected in *The Reception of the Church Fathers in the West,* edited by I Backus, 2 vols. (Leiden: E J Brill, 1997) For an excellent study of Calvin's use of the Fathers, see A N S Lane, *John Calvin: Student of the Church Fathers* (Edinburgh: T and T Clark 1999)

[6] A useful survey and bibliography relating to Augustine and the Reformation can be found in Richard A Muller's article 'Reformation, Augustinianism in the' in *Augustine Through the Ages: An Encyclopedia* (Grand Rapids: Eerdmans, 1999), pp 705-707

[7] Jaroslav Pelikan, The *Christian Tradition: A History of the Development of Doctrine,* 5 volumes (Chicago: Chicago University Press, 1971-89), volume 4, P.21.

[8] See *Works* 3, pp 337-66

[9] *Works* 4, pp. 213-14

[10] One person responded to this paper by reading a passage of scripture to the effect that the gospel is simple and straightforward, the implication being that learning of the kind exemplified by Owen is ultimately not as relevant to the ministry as he (or I) claimed. Interestingly enough, the person chose to read was from a Bible translation – surely a clear concession that the Protestant commitment to a fundamentally simple gospel message and also to the sufficiency and perspicacity of scripture does not obviate the practical desirability, if not necessity, of Bible translations and, presumably, of those with the necessary linguistic and theological skill to produce such. This is essentially the point which Owen's emphasis on learning is intended to establish.

[11] For a good description of the Reformed Orthodox approach to education, see Richard A Muller, 'The Era of Protestant Orthodoxy' in *Theological Education in the Evangelical Tradition,* edited by D G Hart and R Albert Mohler, Jr. (Grand Rapids: Baker, 1996), 103-28.

[12] For further discussion of the eclectic nature of Owen's reading and theology, see *The Claims of Truth,* pp. 1-46

[13] See the discussion in Owen's Latin treatise, *Theologouma Pantodapa* in *Works,* 17, p. 36.

[14] See Francis Junius, *De Vera Theologica,* cap IIII-V in *D. Francisci Junii Opuscula Theologica Selecta* edited by Abraham Kuyper (Amsterdam 1882), pp 51-56. General discussion of the use of the terms in Reformed Orthodoxy can be found in Richard A. Muller, (Grand Rapids: Baker, 1987), pp. 126-36

[15] 17, pp. 38 – 39.

[16] For a good modern discussion of Arminius's theology in relation to Reformed Orthodoxy and classical theism, see Richard Muller, (Grand

Rapids: Baker, 1991);   also Eef Dekker, 'Was Arminius a Molonist?'
1996), 337-52.

[17] The classic statement of Socinian theology is A nineteenth century
edition translated by T. Rees, was published by Longman of London
in 1818.

[18] This is the unspoken assumption throughout Owen's where little
attempt is made to distinguish between the respective positions of
the two schools of thought.

[19] He does allude once to an earlier, apparently unpublished, work on
these themes: see *Works* 13, p. 18.

[20] E.g., his claim that Arminians overturn the eternity and immutability
of God's decrees: *Works*, 13, pp. 14ff. In fact, orthodox Arminians
would not have rejected the eternity and immutability of the decrees,
but rather challenged the Reformed Orthodox understanding of the
relationship between Creator and creatures of which the decrees were
a part. The whole notion of the *scientia media,* or middle knowledge,
which Arminius adopted from the Jesuit Molinists, represented an
attempt (unsuccessful in the eyes of the Reformed, among whom this
writer numbers himself) to hold together eternal divine decrees and
human freedom and responsibility.

[21]   *Works* 11, pp. 12 -13.

[22] The implications of the Arminian positions on providence and sin
are painted with a broad brush in *Works* 10,pp.12 -14 and then elabo-
rated in more detail throughout the work.

[23] See *Works* 17

[24] *Works* p.44.

[25] *Works*, 11, p. 44.

[26] *Works,* 11, pp., 45 -46. He is also dependent upon Augustine for
some of his argumentation: see *Works* 11, pp. 48-49.

[27] *Works 10,* pp. 119 – 120.

[28] *Works* 10, p. 121.

[29] *Works* 10, p. 122.

[30] *Works* 10, p. 122-23.

[31] *Works* 3, p.292.

[32] *Works*10, p.13.

[33] *Works* 10, pp. 90-91.

[34] On this issue see Carl R. Trueman, 'John Owen's *Dissertation on Divine Justice'*, *Calvin Theological Journal* 33 (1998), 87 – 103.

[35] Chapters 3, 4 and 5 outline respectively the work of Father, Son and Holy Spirit but only after Chapter 3 begins with the statement 'The agent in, and the chief author of, this great work of our redemption is the whole blessed Trinity; for all the works which are outwardly of the Deity are undivided and belong equally to each person, their distinct manner of subsistence and order being observed,' *Works* 10, p.163.

[36] *Works* 10, pp. 163 – 179.

[37] *Works* 10, p.219. Owen is responding to the criticisms of *The Death of Death* made by Baxter in his *Aphorismes of Justification* (London 1649). For a more detailed discussion of the points at issue between Owen and Baxter, see *The Claims of Truth*, pp. 199-226.

[38] See *Works* 3, p. 93, where he cites Athanasius, Basil, and Ambrose in support.

[39] See *Works* 3, pp. 91-92.

[40] For an elaboration of this, and detailed references to Owen's arguments, see Trueman, *The Claims of Truth,* pp. 129-39.

[41] Works 3, p. 162.

[42] See *Works,* 3, pp. 170-74; pp. 30-31.

Chapter Three

JOHN OWEN AND THE DOCTRINE OF THE PERSON OF CHRIST

Sinclair Ferguson is currently minister of St George's Tron Church of Scotland, Glasgow and Visiting Professor of Systematic Theology at Westminster Theological Seminary Philadelphia. He is the author of a number of books including *John Owen on the Christian Life*, published by the Banner of Truth.

But had we the tongue of men and angels, we were not able in any just measure to express the glory of this condescension; for it is the most ineffable effect of the divine wisdom of the Father and the love of the Son, – the highest evidence of the care of God towards mankind.
Works 1.330

JOHN OWEN AND THE DOCTRINE OF THE PERSON OF CHRIST

Studying the work of John Owen underlines the principle that when one is able to master the writing of a great theologian, much in contemporary theological literature seems superficial or even superfluous. Certainly that is true of Owen's teaching on the Person of our Lord Jesus Christ, which is worthy of examination for at least these two reasons.

I. A Distinctive Approach

The first is the rather obvious one of the distinctiveness and indeed genius of Owen's approach. There is a considerable amount of literature available today in the area of Christology. But very little of that material comes out of deeply evangelical and biblical convictions and an even smaller proportion breathes the kind of spirit that is characteristic of Owen's work. We find in him the all too rare combination of the sharpness of intellect required in the academy, with the largeness of heart and spirit required for growth in the knowledge of our Lord Jesus Christ.

Of course we should never despise the importance of technical knowledge in the work of the gospel ministry. But merely technical knowledge carries its own danger; a danger Owen managed to avoid. He never lost sight of the fact that the

doctrine of the person of Christ is not so much a doctrine as it is
an exposition of the character of a person.

The personal dimension to his Christology shines through
and indicates the extent to which he placed his intellectual learning in tribute to his pursuit of a personal knowledge of the
person of Jesus Christ.

Owen was well able to write within a polemical context, as
he does in his *Vindiciae Evangelicae*,[1] a critical and devastating
response to John Biddle's version of *The Racovian Catechism*.
He writes at enormous length because he sees the need to
undermine false foundations, and to remove theological
rubble, in order that he might plant Jesus Christ truly in the
hearts and minds of those for whom he writes.

But Christ is not for Owen a subject for technical analysis,
but a person, coming to us 'clothed with his gospel' as Calvin
put it.[2] He is the focus of the Bible's story in order that first he
may be known and, second, that he may be worshipped. There
is constantly in Owen, even when we are in the thick of him
(and some of his writing is dense indeed) a doxological motive
and motif. If we can persevere with his style (which becomes
easier the longer we persevere), he will not fail to bring us to
the feet of Jesus Christ.

II. A Balanced Perspective of Owen's Theology

The second reason why it is helpful to focus on Owen's
Christology, is because doing so helps us to get a more
balanced view of his theology as a whole.

John Owen was a theologian who has been recovered from
obscurity only relatively recently. Until the reprinting of his *Works*
in the mid 1960s, there would have been very few ministers in
the United Kingdom who either possessed a volume of Owen,
or would even have recognised his name. Now thousands do.

Yet probably most attention has been paid to his polemical writing, such as his early work, *The Death of Death in the Death of Christ* (1647), or the striking, and in its own way important, work on the *Mortification of Sin* (1656) . Many readers come to Owen through these works and are perhaps tempted therefore to think that this is Owen in his entirety.

But we need to remember that when he wrote *The Death of Death* in 1647 Owen was only thirty or thirty-one years old. Furthermore the material in *The Mortification of Sin* was not originally prepared for pastors of Christian congregations; in fact it was originally the material of a series of sermons Owen preached to students in the University of Oxford. These were, essentially, addresses to teenagers! He did not view the material as the strong meat for well-tried Christians we see it as. Rather it was basic milk, foundational principles for every Christian believer. It is a sign of the times that we find *The Mortification of Sin* nourishment for serious spiritual athletes!

These two works taken in isolation might therefore give the impression that Owen's great concern was with polemics over the question of the extent of the atonement on the one hand and concern about the mastery of sin in the life of the believer on the other. Deeply concerned though he obviously was about both of these things, he was far more concerned about their foundation in (a) wholesome Trinitarian Theology and (b) knowledge of, trust in and love for the Lord Jesus Christ. Argument without adoration interested him not at all.[3] Focus on sin, without a greater focus on Christ and grace, he recognized, would in fact eventually disable Christian ministry. It could point to the need there is in the human heart but never provide the gospel remedy for it.

For this reason it is an extremely valuable historical-theological exercise for us to focus on the person of Jesus Christ, the centre and goal of all his theology. Indeed, it is not insignificant that the book on which he had been working shortly before his death was *Meditations on the Glory of Christ*.[4] He turned then, instinctively, to the central things of the gospel; and nothing was more central to him than the One who had brought him into fellowship with the Father and with the Holy Spirit.

This theme runs throughout Owen's work, but there are several pieces in his corpus that focus specific attention on Christology.

The first of these is his 1655 publication *Vindiciae Evangelicae*. Here, at the request of the Council of State,[5] he sets out to defend Christian orthodoxy over against the perceived threat of Socinianism. He does this to the extent of some 600 closely argued pages reviewing John Biddle's[6] version of the Racovian Catechism (1605) – probably one of the longest book reviews ever written in the history of the Christian Church!

More positively and broadly, he turned his attention to the person of Christ, and the glory and the beauty of Christ, in what must rank among his greatest works, *Communion with God* (1657).[7] This, like so much else, arose out of his preaching ministry (from around 1650). It is a deeply trinitarian exposition of the character of the Christian life. Owen underlines that the Christian life is at its very root trinitarian in character and that every aspect of our salvation has ultimately to be traced back to the design of the Trinity. Salvation is enjoyed within the context of a distinct communion with each person of the Trinity, with respect to the distinctive aspects of that person's work in the accomplishment of our redemption.[8]

These themes are given more detailed exegetical attention in various places in his mammoth *Exposition of the Epistle to the Hebrews* (1668, 1674, 1680, 1684).[9] Both in the essays ('exercitations') which precede the commentary proper, and in the exposition of the text itself, Owen expounds the centrality of the priesthood of Christ in the work of reconciliation. Then in his great work *Christologia* (1679)[10] he sets out in a more formal way to give expression to the doctrine of Christ's person and then in a more meditative, contemplative fashion in the posthumously published *Meditations on the Glory of Christ* (part one 1684, part two 1689).[11] The production of any one of these volumes would have marked Owen out as a theologian of substance; to have produced all of them marks him as a truly great one. Taken together, they give us real insight into the passion that John Owen held for the person of his Lord Jesus.

This Christological focus can in fact be traced back to Owen's first pastorate in Fordham in Essex. He was installed there in 1642, when he was no more than 26 years old. Three years later, we find him as a young pastor writing to his congregation, deeply burdened by the need to help them to understand the gospel. He is concerned, Paul-like, for their salvation. His desire is to hold back nothing that will be profitable to them and to expose them to the whole counsel of God. As a direct result, for their use – and for the use of the people of God in general he wrote two catechisms.

The title page of this brief work is interesting – it will seem less humorous when we remember that 17th century books did not characteristically have contents pages. Hence the extended title of these catechisms reads: *Two short catechisms, wherein the principles of the doctrine of Christ are unfolded and explained. Proper for all persons to learn before they be admitted to the sacrament of the Lord's Supper and composed for the use of all congregations in general.* The year of their publication (1645) means that they preceded the publication of the Shorter and Larger Catechisms of the Westminster Assembly and helps explain why Owen did not simply use these better known educational tools.

Interestingly, like the Westminster divines and the whole school of Puritan catechists, Owen recognized how important it was as a pastor to have a spiritual concern for the children under his care, and also for those of simple mind, as well as to provide more solid meat for the mature. In both cases Owen was troubled by the fact that many of his parishioners were 'grossly ignorant'[12] of Christ and the gospel. In that sense Owen's burden developed around the same time, and in a manner analogous to, the concern which led Richard Baxter to engage in his great catechetical labours in Kidderminster[13].

In a way that echoes Owen's burden, Baxter tells us in *The Reformed Pastor* why this work is so essential:

> For my part, I study to speak as plainly and movingly as I can, (and next to my study to speak truly, these are my chief studies,) and yet I frequently meet with those that have been my hearers eight or ten years, who know not whether Christ be God or man, and wonder when I tell them the history of his birth and life and death, as if they had never heard it before. And of those who know the history of the gospel, how few are there who know the nature of that faith, repentance, and holiness, which it requireth, or, at least, who know their own hearts? ... I have found by experience, that some ignorant persons, who have been so long unprofitable hearers, have got more knowledge and remorse of conscience in half and hour's close discourse, than they did from ten years' public preaching . . .[14]

With that Baxter-like burden, Owen was driven on to do something, however basic and simple, to help his people understand the character of Christ and the glory of the gospel. In fact, his central burden in these two catechisms is specifically and explicitly the knowledge of Jesus Christ, his person and work.

Interestingly Owen also indicates that he had the intention, unfulfilled as far as there is evidence, of writing further catechisms, which would cover the Lord's Prayer, the Ten Commandments and the articles of the Apostles' Creed. But in these preliminary pieces he focuses on the main essentials: the person of Jesus Christ.

His catechism for younger ones contains 33 questions, eight of which give basic teaching on Christology. The catechism for adults contains 27 chapters, each with several questions. One third of the chapters are on the Trinity, and therefore by definition include aspects of Christology. Chapters 9-14 focus directly on the person of our Lord Jesus Christ. Here in this larger catechism we find a basic framework which comes to fuller expression throughout Owen's future ministry.

1. Jesus Christ is God and man united in one person.
2. Christ fulfils his saving ministry in a two-dimensional way.
   • In his fulfilment of a three-fold office, Prophet, Priest and King
   • In his experience of a two-fold state, the state of humiliation and the state of exaltation.
3. He does this specifically for the sake of the elect.

Already here are the themes he will unravel in his later and greater works; the distinction being that in his later writings he expands on these in a more obviously technical, theological way, in a more clearly expository way, and in a more thorough-going devotional way.

Of course, Owen's writing is historically determined. That is most clearly evident in his *Vindiciae Evangelicae*. But what is most striking about it is his conscious sense that he is expounding a perennial theology, and that the context in which Christology is under attack is essentially the same in every age. Thus when he introduces his exposition in *Christologia*, he does so in terms of Peter's confession and the way in which it immediately came under Satanic attack.[15]

In fact Owen sees this as a kind of paradigm of the whole of church history, coming to expression in different ways and contexts, from the time of Stephen to the time of Constantine in the early church and thereafter constantly repeated over and again.

This in itself helps to bridge the gap between Owen's work in the 17th century and our own times. A common strand runs through all periods of church history – the ongoing antithesis between the kingdom of God and the kingdom of darkness, the heavenly Jerusalem and the earthly Babylon, the powers of light and the powers of darkness. That was the context in which the incarnate Christ was first confessed by Peter; it remains the context in which we seek to witness to Jesus Christ. Consequently, just as the patterns of satanic temptation in Scripture are repeated in our individual lives, so the patterns of satanic attack on the person of Jesus Christ will be repeated in one form or other in every age. These attacks Owen sees as basically three-fold:

1. A theology which denies the role of Christ
2. A rejection of our Lord's divine nature.
3. A rejection of our Lord's hypostatic union; two natures united in one *hypostasis*, or person.

In Owen's own day, these attacks took particularized historical form in:

(i)   Socinianism which denied the deity of Christ.
(ii) Rationalism and Naturalism that denied the necessity of either his deity or his saving humanity.
(iii) The burgeoning 'inner-light' movements which had already troubled the magisterial reformers in the previous century.

These last emphasized the personal indwelling of Christ by the Holy Spirit, rather marginalizing the historical work of Christ in his flesh, on the cross, in the resurrection, in his ascension to the right hand of the Father. Existential experience thus swallowed up *heilsgeschichte* producing a truncated gospel at best and a subjective morass of individually experienced revelations at worst.

If I am not mistaken, although we find ourselves in a different context, we constantly face exactly the same basic critical issues. For this reason, as we try to master Owen's orthodoxy, we discover that his work has an immediate relevance to the times in which we ourselves live.

What, then, is Owen's response? How does he provide a positive exposition of the person of Christ? Here we must confine ourselves to four themes which can be expressed in a series of questions:

1. How does Owen establish the deity of Christ from Scripture?
2. How does Owen think of Christ's relationships within the Trinity?
3. How does Owen understand the nature of the incarnation?
4. Recognising that for Owen the person and work of Christ are inseparable, what does he have to say about the character of his work?

1. THE DEITY OF CHRIST

Owen's approach is generic to orthodox Christology and can be dealt with briefly. He suggests that there are four basic lines of evidence.

1. Many Old Testament testimonies in their original context, clearly describing the one and only God, are applied in the New Testament specifically to Christ. Owen provides several illustrations; but here one will suffice. Psalm 102:25-27 is cited in Hebrews 1:10 and applied specifically to the Son. Thus an Old Testament statement about the character of the deity is equally applicable to the person of the Lord Jesus.

2. The acts that Christ performs are specifically and exclusively divine. Thus in John 1:3 creation is attributed to the *Logos* who is himself specifically excluded from belonging to the category of the created.

3. The attributes Christ possesses are exclusively those of God. For example, in majesty and glory he is one with the Father (John.5:23).

4. Owen notes how some titles given to Jesus in the New Testament are those exclusively titles attributable to the deity.

Here then he is simply following the lines of classical orthodoxy in seeking to establish exegetically from Scripture testimonies to the absolute deity of Jesus Christ.

In his Christology Owen places great stress on the necessity of Christ's deity for the fulfilment of his offices. Here is his Calvin-like consciousness that deity and genuine soteriology belong together in an indivisible way; loosen our grip on one and we inevitably lose our grasp on the other. This is because the deity of Christ relates in Owen's thinking to the character of the obedience of Christ and its power to effect salvation.

We can clarify this point, by analyzing what Owen has to say in five ways:

1. Owen argues that any obedience rendered in a substitutionary way to save sinners, must bring more honour to God's holy character than the dishonour that is reflected on that character by the fall. It must not only bring man back, as it were, to square one in Eden, but forwards to final acceptance

with God. This Owen argues is impossible for a mere man, for the simple reason that God cannot be more pleased with the obedience of one man than he was displeased and dishonoured by Adam's fall. Only an infinite person can give infinite value to an otherwise finite obedience. Furthermore, while one man may act for another man, no single man can offer obedience adequate to substitute for a multitude of men. In order to give that obedience a quality beyond the obedience of one human being, it must be rendered by one who is an infinite person.

2. The obedience of a mere man could not substitute for the failure of others for the simple reason that it would be required of that man for himself: it ... could have no influence at all on the recovery of mankind, nor the salvation of the church. For whatever it were, it would be all due from him, *for himself*, and so could only profit and benefit himself ... He then, that performs this obedience, must be one who was not originally obliged thereunto, on his own account, or for himself.[16] This Owen argues must be a divine person. Every man offering a perfect obedience owes that perfect obedience. To put it crudely, he has no obedience left over to cover anyone else's failure to render that obedience. Supererogation is impossible for mere man. Hence it is necessary, Owen argues, for one who does not owe that obedience to God in terms of the basic relationship between the two, to offer that obedience in the place of others.

3. Given the innumerable multitude of the redeemed and the sins from which they need deliverance, which Owen says are 'next to absolutely infinite',[17] and the fact that these sins are committed against an infinite majesty and therefore have something reductively infinite about them (the terminology is his), only an infinite person could provide satisfaction.

4. Since man cannot fulfil the office of prophet, priest and king, essential for salvation, only a divine person could.

5. Fallen man must be restored to his original state; indeed

Owen argues, it seems 'agreeable unto the glory of the divine excellencies in their operations, that he should be brought into a better and a more honourable condition than that what he had lost'. [18]

But Owen argues, echoing the discussions of the older theologians, anyone who redeems becomes the master of those he redeems. It is therefore unthinkable that we should be redeemed to have any other as our Lord, than the Lord God himself. It was, therefore, morally necessary for redemption to be accomplished by a divine person. To hold that Christ is less than God, to hold that he is a mere man, contradicts a moral principle basic to the logic in the idea of salvation. So redemption is by necessity brought through the infinite wisdom of God in the incarnation of his Son who is himself divine.

Interestingly here the doctrine of God, the doctrine of man's condition and the doctrine of Jesus Christ, are all integrally connected in Owen's theology. Just as pulling a loose thread may unravel an entire garment, so pull one of these strands from the whole fabric of the gospel and we will soon be left with no gospel at all. But Owen's Christology is not limited to this soteriological dimension.

2. RELATIONSHIPS WITHIN THE GODHEAD

What is the relationship of Christ within the Godhead to the other persons of the glorious Trinity?

It is worth repeating frequently in today's climate that Owen, with his high Christology and deep passion for practical Christianity, is also a deeply Trinitarian theologian. This is, in fact, an expression of his profoundly Catholic theology. One might say about Owen – it is certainly evident in his works – that he was first of all a catholic Christian, and then secondly a Puritan, which for him meant simply a consistent Christian.

Owen, like many of his contemporaries, was more conscious than we tend to be of the stream of unity that flows through the history of the church.[19] Of course he was aware of the streams of diversity that flow through the history of theology, and he struggled to contain and sometimes resist them. But as he wrestles with the doctrine of the person of Christ, he understands very clearly the importance of the early Christological and Trinitarian discussions and draws very deeply from them. In his own way he takes these discussions a little further. In his study of *Communion with God* there is, whatever one thinks of his exegesis, an extraordinary further development of the deep seated trinitarianism of both Calvin and the Fathers. It is certainly against the background of this trinitarianism that we should try and understand his Christology.

There is a lesson here, surely, for reformed and evangelical Christians today, not least within the context of the rediscovery of the Puritans. It is all too easy to be caught up in the applicatory end of their theology and lose sight of the grand trinitarian and Christological vision which formed its foundation. It is equally easy to lose sight of their sense of the continuity of the Christian church, warts and all. It was, after all, the reformation, not the incarnation that took place in the 16th century!

Divine Incomprehensibility

How are we to understand the relationship between Christ and the Godhead? Here Owen begins by underlining the important principle of the incomprehensibility of God. Within that context, nothing is more incomprehensible than the way God most fundamentally is in his inner eternal tri-unity. There is a fine statement of this early in his *Christologia*:

> God in his own essence, being, and existence, is absolutely incomprehensible. His nature being immense, and

all his holy properties essentially infinite, no creature can directly or perfectly comprehend them, or any of them. He must be infinite that can perfectly comprehend that which is infinite; wherefore God is perfectly known unto himself only... The subsistence of his most single and simple nature in three distinct persons, though it raises and ennobles faith in its revelation, yet it amazeth reason which would trust to itself   in   the contemplation of it – whence men grow giddy who will own no other guide, and are carried out of the way of truth.[20]

As an aside, Owen's catholicity is illustrated here by his citing with approval Dionysius the pseudo-Areopagite, emphasizing the absolute, total incomprehensibility of God.[21]

As in all areas of his theology, so in this area, we find the necessity of the divine condescension, if the incomprehensible God is to be made known to finite man. Within that context Owen understands the relationship between the Son and the Spirit in terms of Western classical orthodoxy, happily subscribing to the *filioque* clause of Augustinian Christology (that the Spirit proceeds from the Father and from the Son). He argues this in part on the basis of the analogy between the being of God and the revelation of that incomprehensible God in redemptive history. If the incarnation is a genuine revelation of the inner being of God, then, as in redemptive history, so in the very being of God, the Spirit proceeds from both the Father and from the Son.[22]

With respect to the relationship between the Son and the Father, while Owen is committed to the *filioque* clause it is important to say more:

His distinct personality and subsistence was by an internal and eternal act of the Divine Being in the person of the Father, or eternal generation – which is

essential unto the Divine essence – whereby nothing anew
was outwardly wrought or did exist. He was not, he is not, in
that sense, the effect of the Divine wisdom and power of
God but the essential wisdom and power of God himself.[23]

Here Owen is addressing an issue with which Calvin and others
before him had wrestled very deeply. How in our understanding
of the inner relationships in the Godhead, do we emphasize
the Fatherhood of God in relationship to the Son, without inherently suggesting that the Son and correspondingly, the Holy
Spirit, fall into a kind of second (and even third) rank within the
Godhead?

Calvin's way of doing this was to emphasize the autotheistic
nature of the Son. His deity is not derived from the deity of the
Father. Yes, there is a mutual interdependence in terms of
personal relationship; you cannot be a son unless there is a
father, but nor can there be a father, unless there is a son. Calvin
was very insistent that we escape from the incipient
subordinationism of the history of the Christian church by
emphasizing the autotheistic nature of the Son.[24]

While it may be a question how closely Owen follows Calvin's
concerns in this area, he is wrestling with the same issues. While
committed to eternal generation, he emphasises that eternal
generation produces nothing new within, nor anything external
to the being of God. Indeed, the eternally begotten Son is not
to be thought of as the effect of the wisdom and power of God.
He is himself the essential wisdom and power of God himself.
Here, then, Owen seeks to hold together on the one hand the
patristic doctrine of the eternal generation of the Son from the
Father with this Calvinian principle of the absoluteness of the
deity of the Son.

Against that background it is interesting to notice that
particularly in *Vindiciae Evangelicae*, but also elsewhere, Owen
argues that Proverbs 8:22ff, a locus classicus of early

Christological and Trinitarian discussion, actually is a reference to the Son of God.[25] What is said here, he argues, cannot be applied to another and is in fact fulfilled in the description of Christ given in the opening verses of the prologue to John's gospel. The Son and the Father mutually indwell one another in a unity of essence and commune with one another in a distinction of persons. That, in a nutshell, is what Owen is seeking to underline.

Within this eternal relationship, the Father and the Son take counsel together in the fellowship of the Spirit. The axiom *opera trinitatis ad extra sunt indivisa* is consistently maintained. The external actions of God are indivisible in the sense that there is no action of any single person of the Trinity in which the other persons of the Trinity are not simultaneously engaged.

This undergirds not simply Owen's trinitarianism but his Christology in particular. For him the intimacy, the absoluteness of the relationships between the Son and Father in terms of eternal generation, and with the Spirit in terms of eternal procession, ground the principle that when this one comes to save, it is the trinitarian God who is doing the saving. In Christ we discover what God is really like, how God is disposed to us and what God will do for us, because in him we have seen the Father. There is nothing therefore veiled, nothing sinister hidden in God to take us by surprise. This is why it is so very important for Owen, in the context of his doctrine of the incomprehensibility of God, to emphasize that the One who is in the bosom of the Father really has made him known and has the credentials to make him known as fully as we are capable of knowing him, because he is the eternal Son of the eternal Father.

The Son shared in glory with the Father, from all eternity, before all worlds. It is this fellowship, in the communion of the Spirit, that upholds the pillars of the earth, otherwise it would cease to be. It is within this fellowship that both creation and recreation were planned in the context of mutual personal love and delight.[26] Indeed within the trinity there is not only self-existence and self-sufficiency; there is also endless self-delight and satisfaction.

Christology stands as the entrance gate into this communion, for it is Christ who brings us (in intercession and ultimately in reality) to see and then to share in the glory of God. It was to this end that the Son of God assumed our humanity.[27]

This note leads us directly to Owen's focus on the nature of the incarnation.

3. THE NATURE OF THE INCARNATION

Here there are four basic areas which Owen addresses:

1. The appropriateness of the incarnation of the Son.
2. The nature of the incarnation as such.
3. The condescension that is involved in the incarnation
4. The love that is expressed by the incarnation.

We have already reflected on the necessity of the incarnation. When he turns to its nature he raises first a question about the reasons for the second person becoming incarnate.

i. The appropriateness of the Son's incarnation

Why did the Son, in distinction from either the Father or the Spirit, become incarnate? Owen suggests three reasons.[28]

1. Through the fall we have lost acceptance with God and the divine image thereby has been lost. It is therefore, in terms of Hebrews 1:1ff, fitting that the restoration of that lost image should be accomplished by the One who is in himself the

essential image of the God whose image we have 'lost.'

2. We were created to be sons of God with the prospect of a glorious inheritance. It is therefore fitting that the One who is himself the eternal Son of God, through whom all things were made, and for whom they came into existence, the heir of all things, should take upon himself the task of restoring us to sonship with God and bringing us into the divine inheritance.

3. It is fitting that the order of divine subsistence be followed in the order of divine operation. As the Son comes, as it were, from the Father's love in eternal generation, so he is sent to us, in that same love, in the historical event of the incarnation.

So in general terms Owen sees that there is an extraordinary appropriateness about the second person becoming the Redeemer. In particular terms, he finds himself dazzled by the 'infinite wisdom and sovereign counsel of the divine will' that fashioned and fulfilled such a redemptive scheme.[29]

ii. The nature of the incarnation

In the hypostatic union two natures are united in the one divine person of the Son of God. In this act, Owen says, the Son takes our human nature in the womb of the virgin into personal subsistence with himself in an act of power and grace. This principle, easier to state than to analyze, is the bedrock of Owen's Christology. Unless the Son takes human nature into his person, uniting human and divine natures in that one person, that human nature could not really, fully, truly and permanently be his. [30]

We see Owen echoing earlier Christology – the incarnation is not a conversion of one nature into another, but an assumption of human nature by the divine person so that it truly and permanently becomes his own nature. He shares our human nature but in such a way that it becomes the human nature of this particular divine person. The humanity of Jesus is not an appendage. Jesus is not conceived as a divine person with a divine nature and a human nature stuck on, as it were by some kind of incarnational super-glue.

Here we have to confess that we reach the limits of our ability further to conceptualise the implications of biblical teaching. We have no analogy to this. But what Owen rightly insists on is that the human nature of Christ is assumed into union with the person of the Son in such a way that it becomes permanently his. We are not to think that the humanity of Christ becomes redundant on his ascension as though he were, at the end of the day, a divine person with a human bit temporarily added in order to effect the atonement. As becomes clear in his exposition of the high priestly ministry of Christ, human nature is so really and permanently Christ's that he will never exist without it.[31]

There is a broader dimension to this assumption of human nature: in so far as it is an act of God, it is an external act of the trinity. Father, Son and Holy Spirit participate in this action that will bring redemption.

Firstly, it is an act of authoritative designation in which the Father sends the Son.

Secondly, it is an act of divine formation in which the union is the effect of the secret work of the Holy Spirit (Lk. 1:35)

Thirdly, it is an act of sovereign assumption by the Son. He – and not the Father or the Spirit – is the one who assumes the human nature into his own person.[32] But in that act of incarnation with its permanent repercussions, Father and Spirit are engaged and involved, because the redemption of humanity is an act of the eternal Trinity.

What is the effect of this union, the incarnation? Here again Owen stands on the shoulders of the giants of earlier years, giant himself though he proved to be. This union of the Divine person with our human nature by the incarnation takes place without change in the person who assumes the nature. Further, though the natures are distinct, they are not separated but united in the one person. But in that union in the person of the Son, there is no mixture or confusion of the natures. Both natures are possessed personally by the Son, not as it were, accidentally as appendages. This means for Owen that *communicatio idiomatum,* the communication of the properties of the two natures, would better be expressed by the notion of *communio idiomatum,* a communion of the natures in the one Divine person. This, he believes, safeguards three principles fundamental to our salvation:[33]

1. Each nature, united in the person of the Son, preserves its own essential properties, so there is no direct communion between the two in such a way that would lead inevitably to one (the human) becoming subservient to the other nature (the divine). There are two whole, perfect natures, divine and human united in the one person.

2. Each nature therefore operates in accordance with its essential properties:

The divine nature knows all things, upholds all things, rules all things, acts by its presence everywhere. The human nature was born, yielded obedience, died and rose again. But it is the same person, the same Christ who does all these things, the one nature being no less active than the other.[34]

3. The work of Christ then, is not an act of one nature or the other nature, but an act of the whole person (*totus Christus*) in whom these two natures are united.

This principle serves as an hermeneutical key to the way in which we read the New Testament. There some things are spoken of Christ in which what was stated is verified in respect to one nature only; other things are spoken of the person which belong not distinctly or originally to either nature, but to the person as a whole and so on. Thus we interpret such language as men crucifying the Lord of glory or the blood of God being shed for the purchase of the church against the background of an hermeneutic that emerges from a Christology formulated to be consistent with all the data of Scripture. The essential key here is the hypostatic union in which the two natures are not confused, mixed or diminished, but possessed hypostatically in and by the person of the Son.[35]

iii. The condescension of the incarnation

But this is not all. Owen also emphasizes the condescension that is involved in the incarnation. The fact of the incarnation creates mental giddiness in those who seek to understand it, because it is an event without analogy, but also because it expresses an awe-inspiring condescension on the part of God.

There is an infinite distance between the being of God and that of his creatures. He is infinitely self-sufficient while we are lowly and utterly dependent.

> All being is essentially in him, and in comparison there-
> unto all other things are as nothing. And there are no
> measures, there is no proportion between infinite being
> and nothing,– nothing that should induce a regard from
> the one unto the other. Wherefore, the infinite, essential
> greatness of the nature of God, with his infinite
> distance from the nature of all creatures thereby, causeth
> all his dealings with them to be in the way of conde-
> scension or humbling himself.[36]

For Owen, creation is an act of divine humbling. All the more then is redemption in the incarnation an act of divine humbling.

But what is the nature of this humbling? It is not the laying aside of the divine nature. The Son was in the form of God. He participated fully in deity. Yes, he took the form of a servant and was made man but he did not thereby, Owen argues, cease to be God. He did indeed become what he was not, but in doing so he did not cease to be what he ever was. So in his own way, Owen stresses and affirms the so-called *extra-calvinisticum*: while Christ lay in the manger he continued as the Son of God to uphold the universe by his divine power. So there is great condescension, but that does not imply abnegation of his personal being. Nor was the divine nature exchanged for the human, changed into the human, or mixed with the human.[37]

How, then do we describe it? Owen says that the divine nature was veiled during the incarnation. The Son did not cease to be what he always was, but he veiled that which he fully was from all eternity, so much so that far from believing him to be God, his contemporaries did not even believe that he was a good man.

Such was the self-veiling of the Son of God – humbling himself, as Owen says, following scripture, to become a worm and no man. Here he waxes lyrical:

> But had we the tongue of men and angels, we were not able in any just measure to express the glory of this condescension; for it is the most ineffable effect of the divine wisdom of the Father and of the love of the Son, – the highest evidence of the care of God towards mankind. What can be equal unto it? what can be like it?...
>
> We *speak* of these things in a poor low broken manner – we *teach* them as they are revealed in Scripture, – we labour by faith to adhere unto them as revealed; but when we come into a steady, direct view and consideration of the *thing itself*, our minds fail, our hearts tremble, and we can find no rest but in a holy admiration of what we cannot comprehend. Here we are at a loss, and know that we shall be so whilst we are in this world; but all the ineffable fruits and benefits of this truth are communicated unto them that do believe.[38]

God is incomprehensible in himself. There is something incomprehensible in the hypostatic union, something incomprehensible about the condescension of the incarnation. But what we cannot *comprehend* we may nevertheless *apprehend.* And so we have nothing to fear from either the will or the power of God because both of these are exercised towards us in Christ by means of the condescension of the incarnation.

iv. The love expressed in the incarnation

It is clear now that the incarnation is a mighty expression of the love of God, set against the backcloth of the Father's electing grace to the unworthy and the defiled. Christ's first act of love, Owen says, arises as he views us in our sinfulness and under judgment. It is an act of pity and compassion. He viewed us as recoverable in the light of his death and his love delights in what we will become by his grace.

Against that background Owen sees the way of salvation being proposed to the Son in the covenant of redemption.[39] This was a task of immense difficulty, requiring the Son to assume our humanity, and requiring of him an unparalleled act of love which would at the same time be an act of his whole being in obedience to his Father. Nevertheless the Son displays this love with respect to both natures, each acting in accordance with its own distinct properties. His love is always the love of one and the same person, never of merely one or other nature.

This brings us to our fourth major emphasis.

4. THE CHARACTER OF CHRIST'S WORK

Here we move seamlessly from considering the person of Christ in his work to considering the work of Christ as a revelation of his person. We must limit our focus to one aspect of Owen's teaching which particularly helps us grasp the magnitude of his

Christological vision.

What is the character of Christ's work? In the history of the church there has been a tendency to play off against each other various theories and interpretations of the atonement as though the work of Christ were one-dimensional. Owen, by contrast, while stressing the significance of the substitutionary nature and obedience-orientation of the atonement, also recognises that the work of Christ is multi-dimensional in form and multivalent in function. But the background to every aspect of it is that it is an act of divine recapitulation in which Jesus Christ comes as the Second Man and the Last Adam, first to restore individual sinners and an entire people to fellowship with God, and then to bring a restored, reconstituted and glorious universe into being – one that surpasses creation in its original form. It is particularly fascinating to see the way in which Owen here resurrects and seeks to perfect biblically a motif normally associated with the early church father, Irenaeus.[40]

Owen expounds this against the background of Paul's teaching in Ephesians 1:20-22 and Colossians 1:15-20. He is convinced from his reading of Scripture that in the original creation God brought into being two families distinct from each other:

1. a family in heaven of archangels, angels, cherubim
      and seraphim, and
2. a family on earth consisting of human beings.

These two families, distinct from each other, were united only in so far as their obedience was owed to God himself.[41] But (as Owen reads Scripture), part of the family of heaven and all of the family on earth, sinned and fell. As a consequence God cut off the angels who had fallen and, by contrast, decreed to preserve the unfallen angels and to save a remnant of those who had fallen in the human family. His plan was to accomplish this now, not in terms of the original creation, but in terms of a new creation in which those two families would be united as one. One part (angelic) would be preserved from sinning, the other (human) part delivered from the guilt and power and eventually the very presence of sin.

This, for Owen, is the vision of which Paul speaks when he envisages everything in heaven and earth being headed up in Christ. Thus both the family in heaven and the family on earth are indebted to the incarnation, death, resurrection, exultation, heavenly ascension and final return of the incarnate Son – albeit not in identical ways. Christ thus comes to save sinners, to restore the universe to its stability and to fill it with glory, and hence to bring the two families together as one glorious fellowship of which he himself is the head.

How does the Son of God do this? He does it, Owen argues, *principally* by atonement as obedience. He became obedient to the law of God as he discharged his three-fold office in terms of a substitution of his obedience for our disobedience. His obedience was perfect. It was notably accomplished, not in the context of an unfallen world, but in the context of a fallen, decaying and disintegrating world. That contrast is emblematized in biblical history by the fact that while Adam failed in a garden, Jesus was tempted in a wilderness. By contrast with Eden, the garden in which Adam met with God in the evening, it was in dark Gethsemane that Jesus met with God, experiencing it as a place of crying and tears.

It is against this background of a cosmic perspective, the *anakephalaiosis*, that the work of Christ is seen to be glorious by believers, and the majesty of Christ himself becomes clearer.

How glorious is the Lord Christ on this account, in the eyes of believers. When Adam had sinned, and thereby eternally, according unto the sanction of the law, ruined himself and all his posterity, he stood ashamed, afraid, trembling, as one ready to perish for ever, under the displeasure of God. Death was that which he had deserved, and immediate death was that which he looked for. In this state the Lord Christ in the promise comes unto him, and says, Poor creature! how woful is thy condition! how deformed is thy appearance! What is become of the beauty, of the glory of that image of God wherein thou wast created? how hast thou taken on thee the monstrous shape and image of Satan? And yet thy present misery, thy entrance into dust and darkness, is no way to be compared with what is to ensue. Eternal distress lies at the door. But yet look up once more, and behold me, that thou mayest have some glimpse of what is in the designs of infinite wisdom, love, and grace. Come forth from thy vain shelter, thy hiding place. I will put myself into thy condition. I will undergo and bear that burden of guilt and punishment which should sink thee eternally into the bottom of hell. I will pay that which I never took; and be made *temporally* a curse for thee, that thou mayest attain unto *eternal* blessedness. To the same purpose he speaks unto convinced sinners, in the invitation he gives them to come unto him.[42]

This, then, says Owen, is the Lord Jesus Christ who is set before us in the gospel. The Son of God, in infinite grace, laid aside infinite dignity in an act of infinite condescension revealing infinite love and all with a view to producing infinite glory.

The knowledge of the person of Jesus Christ was never an academic matter for Owen. On the last day of his life he was visited at home in the (then) 'quiet village of Ealing'[43] by his friend William Payne. Payne was seeing his *Meditations on the Glory of Christ* through publication, and called to tell him the work was beginning to roll off the press. But Owen's eyes were already seeing beyond his own meditations. He responded,

I am glad to hear it; but, O brother Payne! The long wished

for day is come at last in which I shall see that glory in
another manner than I have ever done, or was capable of
doing in this world.[44]

Owen saw a great deal of that glory in this world. His deathbed
testimony simply underlines how much more glorious he
expected the actual reality to be than his efforts to express it.

It would be to miss the whole point of Owen's teaching if we
failed to ask ourselves the obvious questions arising from any
reading of his Christology. But perhaps it is important to spell
them out simply:

1. How seriously do I pursue the knowledge of Christ?
2. How central is Jesus Christ in our preaching and worship?
3. How can it be – if these are the riches of Christ – when
   we too possess these riches, that the church today is
   so silent and embarrassed about its Saviour?

Notes

[1] 'Vindiciae Evangelicae', Oxford, 1655, in W.H. Goold, ed., *The Works of John Owen*, Edinburgh 1850-53, vol. 12:1-590 is an exhaustive critique of Socinianism.

[2] *Institutes of the Christian Religion*, III.2.6.

[3] *Works* 12.52

[4] This work ('Meditations' was Owen's own description) was written originally for his own benefit and then for the encouragement of a private group who listened to him. It was first published in 1684, in the year following his death.

[5] The Council of State was formed after the British Isles were declared a republic and became a Commonwealth. It was the executive body of the new one-chamber Parliament. It was chaired by the Lord Protector Oliver Cromwell.

[6] Biddle (1616-1662), an Oxford graduate and a teacher was a central figure in spreading Socinian anti-trinitarian views in England. He spent much of his life in jail as a result.

[7] *Works* 2, pp1-274.

[8] Sometimes referred to as the doctrine of appropriations.

[9] Volumes 18-24 in the original Goold edition of the *Works*, Edinburgh 1854-55.

[10] *Works* 1, 1-272.

[11] Part 1 was published in 1684, Part 2 in 1689. *Works* 1. 274-463.

[12] The words are from his dedicatory letter to the catechisms; cf. *Works* 1. p.465.

[13] R.Baxter, *The Reformed Pastor* (1656) chronicles this vividly and at length.

[14] *The Reformed Pastor*, ed. and abridged W. Brown (1829), reprinted Edinburgh, Banner of Truth Trust, 1974, p.196.

[15] *Works* 1.29

[16] *Works* 1.201

[17] Ibid.

[18] *Works* 1.203

[19] Thus for all his closer affinity with Calvin than with Augustine, like other major Puritan figures, Owen cites the bishop of Hippo several times more frequently than he does the reformer of Geneva. And references to the Fathers punctuate many of his writings. His extensive personal library included many of their works.

[20] *Works* 1.65

[21] Dionysius the pseudo-Areopagite was a mystical, neo-platonic, and, probably, Syrian theologian of the 5th or 6th centuries. Until the Renaissance and Reformation he was often assumed to be Dionysius the council member of the Areopagus who became a Christian (Acts 17:34).

[22] See e.g. *Works* 2.226; 3.60-61.

[23] *Works* 1.45

[24] B.B. Warfield's magisterial study remains the best guide here. See *The Works of Benjamin B Warfield,* Oxford University Press, New York, 1931, vol.5, *Calvin and Calvinism,* pp.189-284.

[25] See e.g. *Works* 1.54ff; 2.390; 12.243-5, 501; 19.58-60 [Hebrews vol.2].

[26] See e.g. *Works* 1.144ff.

[27] *Works* 1. 287ff.

[28] *Works* 1.218-220

[29] *Works* 1.218

[30] *Works* 1.223-235

[31] *Works* 21.422-424

[32] *Works* 1.225

[33] *Works* 1.234

[34] *Works* 1.234

[35] *Works* 1.234-235

[36] *Works* 1.324

[37] *Works* 1.229

[38] *Works* 1.330

[39] Sometimes called 'the covenant of the Mediator or Redeemer.' See *Works* 19.78; 22.230. See further, S.B. Ferguson, *John Owen on the Christian Life,* Edinburgh, the Banner of Truth Trust, 1987, pp.25-27.

[40] Irenaeus, bishop of Lyons during the late second century, expounds his teaching on the reversal of Adam's fall in the incarnation and obedience of Christ in various sections of his *Against Heresies.*

[41] *Works* 1.369-70

[42] *Works* 1.341-2.

[43] *Works* 1.CII

[44] *Works* 1.CIII

Chapter Four

JOHN OWEN AND THE DOCTRINE OF THE HOLY SPIRIT

Sinclair Ferguson is currently minister of St George's Tron Church of Scotland, Glasgow and Visiting Professor of Systematic Theology at Westminster Theological Seminary Philadelphia. He is the author of a number of books including *John Owen on the Christian Life*, published by the Banner of Truth.

Oftentimes they go for water to the well, and are not able to draw ... they seek to promises for refreshment, and find no more savour in them than in the white of an egg; but when the same promises are brought to remembrance by the Spirit the Comforter, who is with them and in them, how full of life and power are they!
Works 11.347

JOHN OWEN AND THE DOCTRINE OF THE HOLY SPIRIT

The Martyn Lloyd-Jones Memorial Lecture 2000

The doctrine of the Holy Spirit was of crucial theological importance to John Owen. His great work *Pneumatologia* covers two volumes of his *Works* in the Goold Edition,[1] almost 1200 pages in all. Its size and comprehensive vision give eloquent expression to his sense of the need for a thorough biblical exposition and a comprehensive theology of the Holy Spirit. The work – really a series of nine books – began to be published in 1674 when Owen was fifty-eight years old. The final volumes appeared posthumously in 1693. It represents the mature mind of a very great systematic thinker who was also an outstanding pastoral theologian.

Owen himself recognised the historical significance in his work. It is easy to forget that a man born in 1616 could theoretically have known an elderly man who, in his youth, had listened to the preaching of John Calvin. The birthday of the Reformation was not yet a century past. And central to that revolution had been a recovery of an understanding and experience of the role of the Holy Spirit in the church and in the individual. Indeed Edmund Campion, the famous Jesuit missionary to England,[2] said on one occasion that the great dividing line between Rome and Geneva lay along the axis of the doctrine of the person and work of the Holy Spirit.

Such a statement from a Counter-Reformation figure like Campion simply confirmed what especially Calvin (and later Owen and others) recognised. The Roman Catholic Church had sequestered for the church's magisterium, priesthood and sacramental administration what properly belonged exclusively to the Holy Spirit. He alone can bring men to Christ, keep them in Christ, and assure them that through faith they belong to Christ and will be finally saved by God's free grace. In keeping with this, the learned Robert Bellarmine, the greatest theologian of the Roman Catholic Counter-Reformation movement, wrote that assurance is the greatest of all Protestant heresies.[3]

Against this historical background John Owen became increasingly conscious of the strategic importance of expounding the ministry of the Holy Spirit. He does this in essentially three dimensions, working simultaneously on several fronts.

I. Constructive exposition

First of all Owen wants constructively and comprehensively to expound the ministry of the Holy Spirit within a solid Biblical theology. He introduces his work on this note: 'I know not any who ever went before me in this design of representing the whole economy of the Holy Spirit with all his adjuncts, operations, and effects'.[4]

Owen was very conscious that he was constructively contributing to the theology, not only of his own era, but also of the entire Christian Church. Of course a number of the Church Fathers had written on the doctrine of the Holy Spirit,[5] but their focus tended to be on his personal divine identity. Owen's vision was larger as well as being more obviously orientated to soteriology and its pastoral implications. And it is out of that context that he wrote the monumental exposition of the Holy Spirit with which we are familiar.

II. Defensive polemic

But not only did Owen work constructively; he also engaged in polemic. He seeks to expound and define biblical teaching over against a whole series of errors:

1. Over against Rome and the way in which it had usurped the Spirit's role and replaced it with the magisterial authority of the church and the ministry of the sacraments.
2. Over against the increasing influence of a rationalism which regarded Christianity merely as an external behavioural pattern of which the natural man is capable.
3. Over against those forms of spirituality that stressed the immediacy of the Spirit's presence in the giving of continuing revelation. That had already been an ongoing burden to Calvin; if anything it had become a more critical issue by the time of Owen.

The theology of the main line reformers had sought to stress the harmony of the Spirit with the word. Over against this, elements in the radical reformation tended to bypass the written word of Scripture and claimed the immediate revelation and leading of the Holy Spirit. Calvin himself had complained about the impossibility of discussion with people who punctuate every paragraph they utter with references to what the Spirit has told them.[6]

It is sometimes said, by way of whimsical summary of the Reformation's teaching, that if we emphasise the word without the Spirit then we will *dry up*, if we emphasise the Spirit without the word we will *blow up* (!); but if we emphasise the Spirit and the Word we will *grow up*. Owen had his own version of this: 'He that would utterly separate the Spirit from the word had as good burn his Bible.'[7]

It is worth noting in passing that the context in which Owen was seeking to build a biblical doctrine of the Holy Spirit was not dissimilar to the context in which we minister the word of God today: a rationalism that denies the reality of the supernatural and in its ecclesiastical garb sees either liturgy or decency as equivalent to Christianity; an increasing interest in mystical and sacerdotal religion; a context in which a healthy orthodox evangelical biblicism is giving way to a denial of the sufficiency of Scripture interpreted and applied by the Spirit, replacing written revelation with immediate revelation as the canon of the Christian's decision-making process. If we can get revelation from God directly, it is psychologically inevitable that we will find less enthusiasm for serious Bible study! There is, therefore, an impressive relevance about what Owen said so many generations ago.

III. Experimental Focus

Owen also writes with a concern for Christian experience. He had, after all, a deep personal reason to expound the role of the ministry of the Holy Spirit in the believer.

One of the axioms that Owen returns to again and again as a preacher of the gospel is that there is a difference between the knowledge of the truth and the knowledge of the power of the truth. That was a distinction carved out of personal experience. For he himself had possessed a knowledge of the truth since childhood (his own father was a minister with Puritan leanings). Yet he had at one time a deep consciousness that he lacked real experience of the power of the truth of which he had so much knowledge.[8] For the later Owen it became

axiomatic that it is the presence of the Spirit of God that trans-
forms our bare knowledge of the truth into our experience of
the power of the truth. He lived and breathed for this. As David
Clarkson[9] would say later, in his funeral address after Owen's
death, it was for the promotion of Spirit-given holiness that all
of John Owen's significant intellectual powers were laid in tribute at the feet of his Lord Jesus Christ.[10]

There is an embarrassment of riches to be explored in Owen's
doctrine of the Holy Spirit. Here we must restrict ourselves to
two central aspects of his thought. Taken together they will help
us to catch the flavour of his approach to the role and power of
the Holy Spirit in the life of the believer. He explores the relationship of the Spirit first to Christ, and then to the believer.

Although Owen gave unequal attention to these themes in
terms of length of treatment, they are integrally related in his
theology, the first providing the framework for the second.

1. THE HOLY SPIRIT IN COMMUNION WITH CHRIST

Evangelical theology has long had a tendency to leapfrog over
redemptive history and head directly to personal experience of
salvation. Put in technical terms, it has often ignored the significance of the being and activity of God in favour of subjective
experience of God, bypassing *historia salutis* in favour of an
interest in *ordo salutis*.[11]

Owen manfully resisted that tendency. In his pneumatology
in particular he emphasises that, in order to understand the
significance of the work of the Holy Spirit, we must first explore
his relationship to the life and ministry of our Lord Jesus Christ.

Owen refers in this connection to the prophetic Psalm 45:
'You love righteousness and hate wickedness, therefore God
your God has set you above your companions by anointing
you with the oil of joy' (Ps. 45:6-7). He raises two questions

with (in his view) obvious answers. (i) About whom does the psalmist speak? Answer: the use of these words in Hebrews 1: 9 makes it clear that he speaks of the Lord Jesus Christ. (ii) Of what does the psalmist speak when he says: 'God your God has set you above your companions by anointing you with the oil of joy'? Answer: the words of John 3: 34 make clear that he is looking forward to the anointing of Jesus Christ with the Spirit without measure.

Owen's understanding of the believer's experience of the Holy Spirit rests upon this foundation. Jesus Christ, who gives the Spirit to his people on the day of Pentecost, and who bestows the same gift on all those who trust him, does so as the one upon whom that Spirit was first and foremost bestowed.

Thus Owen understands that Jesus was the recipient and bearer of the Spirit both *prior to* our becoming the recipients of the Spirit and also *with a specific view to* our reception of the Spirit. Furthermore, the relationship formed between the divine Spirit and the incarnate Mediator is determinative of the character of the ministry of the Holy Spirit to all believers. So, says Owen, Christ, who was conceived under the aegis of the Holy Spirit was, from the moment of conception in his mother's womb right through to his resurrection and exaltation, also borne by the Spirit, and in turn bore the Spirit in order that after his ascension he might give the very Spirit who was upon him to all who believe in him.

Owen sees four critical stages of our Lord's relationship to the Holy Spirit in connection with his ministry to him as the Messiah.

1. The Incarnation

Wherever we turn in Owen's theology we encounter various applications of the patristic axiom: *opera Trinitatis ad extra sunt indivisa.*[12] This is certainly true of his doctrine of the incarnation proper. The Father prepares a body for his Son and sends him. Simultaneously the Son takes hold not of the seed of angels but of the seed of Abraham (Heb. 2:16). This work of the Father and this act of the Son take place in and through the power of the Holy Spirit.

Our Lord's conception has all the characteristic marks of the Spirit's work. As the Spirit overshadowed the first work of creation, and at Pentecost overshadowed the first moments of re-creation, so when the author of that first creation became the head of the new creation in the womb of the virgin Mary, the Holy Spirit again acted as the executive of the Godhead. It was through the Holy Spirit that the Holy One was conceived in the virgin's womb. By that same act in the mystery of virgin conception, the humanity which the Son assumed in the womb of the Virgin Mary was sanctified. Thus the 'thing' (Luke 1:35 A.V.) that was conceived in her was simultaneously fully human and fully holy.[13]

Thus by the power of the Spirit our Lord, the second person of the Trinity, became the second man and the last Adam.[14] The striking result of this, for Owen, is that here uniquely, by this work of God's grace, there emerges one among us in whom grace and nature meet in harmony.

2. The Ministry

Owen further develops this train of thought by moving from the Spirit's ministry in Jesus's conception and birth to his ministry throughout the course of his life. For Owen it is axiomatic that although our Lord lived in the power of the Spirit, he 'acted grace as a man',[15] that is as a man, fully man, truly man and in every aspect of his humanity. This is expounded in two ways:

i. Jesus' Human Development

The reality of Christ's humanity carries with it an important implication. It means that there is, by definition, a progress in our Lord's humanity and correspondingly progress in his holiness – not from sin to holiness as such, but from *holiness* to *holiness*, in a manner commensurate with the natural progress within his humanity. This is implied in the statement of Luke 2: 52 that as he grew in stature and in favour with men, he also grew in favour with God as he grew in wisdom.[16]

As Owen points out from the messianic prophecies (Isa.11:1-3), this wisdom is the distinguishing feature of the individual who is full of the Holy Spirit. As his natural capacities developed so the Spirit of God worked in the Lord Jesus, gradually and incrementally training him in the development of perfect godliness at each stage of his life.

In this sense Jesus obeyed the law of God perfectly and did so in the power of the Holy Spirit, 'naturally' in the sense of 'in a fully and truly human way.' There was nothing inhuman, a-human or superhuman about the obedience of Jesus. The Spirit of God led him into a full, perfect and 'natural' humanity. Correspondingly the mind of the Lord Jesus – under the influence of the Holy Spirit – was illumined by the Scriptures to guide him on each step of his way, as he lived in the general obedience to God required of man as creature and the specific obedience to God required by Jesus as Messiah:

> In the representation, then, of things anew to the human nature of Christ, the wisdom and knowledge of his human nature was *objectively* increased, and in new trials and temptations he *experimentally* learned the new exercise of grace. And this was the constant work of the Holy Spirit on the human nature of Christ.[17]

To put Owen's point in blunt terms: the Messiah who died on the cross did not come immediately from heaven to the cross. Rather, he developed from his (literally) embryonic condition in the womb, through the natural processes of growth, accompanied by the development of holiness in the power of the Spirit, to become a mature man in his thirties. In him uniquely, ongoing growth in obedience and in the fruit of the Spirit were perfectly commensurate with the natural development of all human characteristics:

> This was the constant work of the Holy Spirit on the human nature of Christ: He dwelt in him in fullness; for he received not him by measure. And continually, upon all occasions, he gave out of his unsearchable treasures grace for exercise in all duties and instances of it. From hence was Jesus habitually holy, and from hence did he exercise holiness entirely and universally in all things.[18]

ii. The Public Ministry

Jesus grew strong in the Holy Spirit during the hidden years from twelve to thirty. But at his baptism, according to Owen, he entered into the fulness of the Spirit, not for progress in holiness, but to be equipped to fulfil his messianic ministry. The baptismal descent of the Spirit was specifically related to a new stage in his ministry as Messiah, not to a new stage in his humanity in its ordinary development. Gifts were now given to him by the Spirit, in order that he might don the armour of God to engage in the ages-old conflict between the kingdom of God and the powers of darkness.[19] In his battle against Satan he took the sword of the Spirit, which is the word of God, in order to overcome the kingdom of darkness. In his use of Scripture he simultaneously obeyed his Father, maintained his own integrity and, under the Spirit's guidance caused Satan to flee.

Already then, at this stage in Jesus' ministry, Owen is hinting that the ministry of the Spirit in the life of our Lord will serve as the paradigm for the ministry of the Spirit in the life of the believer. Here the great axiom in Calvin's theology, that word and Spirit must never be separated, is given very practical expression. The Lord Jesus himself as second Man becomes a living embodiment of obedience to and fulfilment of the word of God.

3. The Sacrifice

Here, for Owen, the key text is Hebrews 9: 13, 14. It was 'through the eternal S(s)pirit' that our Lord 'offered himself unblemished [as a sacrifice] to God.' There is an expressed contrast here. The sacrifice of the blood of bulls and goats was inherently inadequate to take away the sins of human beings. Christ, by contrast, offered himself, and did so through the eternal Spirit.

There is an exegetical crux to be resolved here. Is the referent to the human spirit of Jesus or to the Holy Spirit? Owen thinks the latter and emphasises two things. First, the explicit contrast between Old Testament sacrifices and the sacrifice of Christ: 'the blood of bulls and goats' – 'offered himself'. The former sacrifices were made on the altar of tabernacle and temple; the latter, the sacrifice of Christ, was made, says Owen, not on a material altar but by the Holy Spirit.[20]

It is interesting to see what Owen is doing here with the text. He is setting the blood of bulls and goats within its redemptive historical context of temple sacrifice as type, and seeing the fulfilment of it, the antitype, in the sacrifice of Jesus. On what altar did Jesus make himself the sacrifice? Owen believes that the author of Hebrews (in his view, Paul) is teaching us that no earthly altar can support the weight of an infinite sacrifice. Only the Eternal Spirit could bear the weight of an eternal person bearing the weight of human sin.

Owen does not mean to deny the Protestant watchword that Calvary is our only altar. But he wishes to stress that it is the Holy Spirit alone who is capable of bearing the weight of an infinite sacrifice in order that it might be placed before God. While fire consumed the whole burnt offerings of the temple, Christ's true and final sacrifice expressed the kindling of the Spirit, the zeal for the glory of God that consumed him.[21]

But further, Owen goes on to say, these words explain more pointedly the nature of the Spirit's ministry in Jesus' sacrifice.

1. He must, first of all, be seen as supporting Jesus in his decision to offer himself to the Father throughout the whole course of his life, with a view to his sacrificial death.

2. He must be seen as the Spirit who sustained Jesus as he came near to the gate of the temple when, in the Garden of Gethsemane, he caught sight at close range of the bloody altar that awaited him.

3. That same Spirit held Jesus up in the breaking of his heart and the engulfing of his soul as he experienced the dereliction of Calvary.[22]

But even here Owen is not finished. He adds a deeply moving touch by asking the question: If, on the cross, our Lord Jesus Christ committed his spirit into the hands of his Father, to what did he commit his body? *Externally*, says Owen, his lifeless body was guarded by the holy angels, mounted as a watch over the garden tomb. But internally the Spirit preserved it from corruption in the darkness of Joseph's tomb, just as it had been preserved from corruption by that same Spirit in the darkness of the womb of the Virgin Mary.[23] From womb to tomb the devotion of the Spirit to the enfleshed Son was constantly evident. This brings us to a fourth aspect of our Lord's communion with the Spirit.

4. The Exaltation

The ministry of the Spirit in the life of our Lord is also revealed at the point of our Lord's exaltation. Here again Owen notes that the external works of the Trinity are indivisible. The Father raises up the Son; and yet the New Testament also teaches that the Son has power to lay down his life and to take it up again. Here Father and Son are together harmoniously active in the exaltation of the resurrection.

But Owen also notes the New Testament hints at the role of the Holy Spirit in the resurrection exaltation of our Lord.[24] The Spirit declared him Son of God with power through the resurrection; the Spirit thereby vindicates him. Nor is this merely a work of resuscitation; it is a work of transformation and of glorification. As Owen puts it, 'He who first made his nature *holy*, now made it *glorious.*'[25] Not only then from womb to tomb is the Spirit present powerfully in the life of our Lord, but, we might say, from womb to glory the Spirit has been the companion of every moment of his human experience.

What is the significance of this theology?

For Owen, this communion between the Spirit and the Son, the Son and the Spirit, gives expression to a basic New Testament principle: the Spirit is not to be known apart from Christ, just as Christ cannot be known by us apart from the Spirit. This is true for two reasons:

First, the source of the Spirit's ministry in the believer is Jesus Christ. Jesus the bearer of the Spirit has now become the bestower of the Spirit. And he is the bestower of the Spirit as the One who has been the bearer of the Spirit. To put it otherwise, it is the very Spirit he has borne as incarnate *and no other*, whom he pours out upon the church on the day of Pentecost.

Second, because of this intimate relationship between the Spirit and the incarnate Son, the identity in which the Spirit comes to the church and the believer is defined by his intimate relationship to the life of the incarnate Saviour. The Spirit is able to take from what is Christ's and make it known to us, because he has been dynamically active in Christ's incarnate life and ministry. He is intimately knowledgeable about Christ. He is therefore able to bring to believers, from the now-exalted Christ, all the riches of the grace embodied in his humanity. It follows inevitably that, if this is the dynamic of his ministry, its goal will inevitably be to transform us into the likeness of Christ. The Spirit takes from the fulness of Christ and brings it to us in order that we may be transformed by his ministry into the likeness of Christ. This brings us to our second major consideration.

2. THE HOLY SPIRIT IN COMMUNION WITH THE BELIEVER

In his Farewell Discourse, Jesus said that it was to the advantage of his disciples that he was leaving them; in his place the Spirit would come (John. 16:11). With an eye to Roman Catholic polemic, shrewdly and somewhat amusingly Owen notes that reformed believers possess two things Rome denies they have. They have the Vicar of Christ on earth and a priceless relic given to them by Christ – the Holy Spirit! He comes to us shaped, as it were, by Jesus' history and ministry. He is in that sense another comforter (*allos parakletos*). Having been with Jesus throughout his life and ministry, he can be subjectively to us all that Jesus objectively was. He can bring to us from the fulness of Christ and, therefore, minister to us as the Vicar of Christ. His presence in our lives is the great relic that the Lord Jesus has bestowed upon the church.

Owen is one of relatively few theologians who have spelled out the implications of Peter's words on the Day of Pentecost: 'exalted to the right hand of God he has received from the Father the promised Holy Spirit' (Acts 2:33).[26]

Explaining the significance of that event Peter says – speaking about Christ – that having been exalted to the right hand of God, he has received from the Father the promised Holy Spirit (Acts 2:33). Theologians have characteristically noted that Christ is exalted to the right hand of the Father and then pours out the Spirit upon the Church. What they have not noted is the relationship between these two events: at the point of exaltation a further transaction takes place within the Godhead between the Father and the Son, one prophesied by Jesus: '*I will ask the Father* and he will give you another comforter to be with you for ever' (John. 14:16). Owen recognises here, the fulfilment of a whole raft of prophecies that run through the Old Testament Scriptures, from God's promise to Abraham that in his seed the nations would be blessed (Gen.12: 3), to, for example Psalm 2:8: 'Ask of me and I will give you the nations for your inheritance.'

Here the covenant between the Father and the Son reaches its climactic fulfilment. The Son, having fully obeyed the stipulations of the covenant of redemption, now, on his ascension, returns to the Father and says, 'Father you promised ... You promised that if I were obedient to death, then I would be exalted and rewarded with a people.' Owen held that now, on his ascension, our Lord Jesus asks for this, in the understanding that only the outpouring of his Spirit can bring it to pass. Only the One who has dwelt upon Jesus can produce a people like Jesus. For this reason, like the true and wise Solomon he is, on his coronation at the right hand of the Father, Jesus asks for the Holy Spirit.

It is upon this gift of the Spirit, asked for, received, and bestowed by Christ, that virtually everything in the Christian life depends. The Spirit is the agent of illumination, the author of regeneration, the sanctifier, the author of spiritual gifts, the Christian's consolation in affliction.[27]

What then is the nature of this ministry of the Spirit? Owen has two ways of answering that question. The first is what we might call the biographical way, tracing the dimensions of the Spirit's ministry in applying redemption in terms of the *ordo salutis*. He uses the example of Augustine as a paradigm of how the Spirit works in bringing us to saving faith.[28]

The second answer, on which we will concentrate, is thematic. Here Owen traces not so much the pattern of the application of redemption as the chief characteristics of the believer's communion with the Spirit. He believes there are four ways in which the Spirit evidences his presence and power in communion with the believer: indwelling, unction, earnest and seal. For all practical purposes, he regards unction and earnest as aspects of indwelling. Thus we can reduce his perspective to two essential aspects: indwelling and sealing.

1. Indwelling of the Spirit

The Spirit indwells every believer mysteriously.[29] But he does so, Owen recognises, personally as the Spirit of Christ.[30] Owen makes a distinction, which he shares with other Puritan writers on this theme, between the indwelling of the Holy Spirit as the Spirit of holiness and his self-manifestation as Comforter. The former is a constant ministry. The Spirit is always, under all circumstances, at all times making us holy. He uses every situation – joys, trials, successes and failures – to conform us to the image of God's Son.

But the manifestation of the Spirit as Comforter, Owen argues, is a ministry of an intermittent character. While he acts in all circumstances to sanctify us he does not similarly act to bring us a conscious sense of the comforts of the gospel.[31] The point is an important one for Owen, for the simple reason that he believes we need to distinguish between the indwelling of the Spirit (a constant) and the manner in which he manifests that identity in and to the consciousness of the individual believer (a variable). One obvious implication of this arises in the doctrine of assurance – in the distinction between assurance that is provided in the gift of Christ and the manifold sense of it in the believer's conscience.

Nevertheless, Owen holds that the indwelling of the Holy Spirit brings with it several distinct blessings.

i. The Spirit comes to give the believer direction and guidance[32] –a guidance that is moral and extrinsical, in the sense that the Spirit gives it to us objectively in the word he has indited; a guidance that is internal and efficient as the Holy Spirit illuminates our understanding of the Scriptures. In addition he enables us to embrace the teaching Scripture gives us as well as the providences that govern our lives under the sovereign hand of God.

This, for Owen, is tantamount to what the New Testament means when it speaks of the anointing of the Spirit (1 John 2: 20, 27). Christian believers do not need teachers in this context because they have received the anointing.

ii. The Spirit comes to give support; in terms of Romans 8: 26ff, he helps us in our infirmities[33].

He does this by the application of the Scriptures, illumining their force, relevance and practical application to us:

> And this he doth every day. How often, when the spirits of the saints are ready to faint within them, when straits and perplexities are round about them, that they know not what to do, nor whither to apply themselves for help or supportment, doth the Spirit that dwelleth in them bring to mind some seasonable, suitable promise of

Christ, that bears them up quite above their difficulties and distractions, opening such a new spring of life and consolation to their souls as that they who but now stooped, yea were almost bowed to the ground, do stand upright, and feel no weight or burden at all! Oftentimes they go for water to the well, and are not able to draw; or, if it be poured out upon them, it comes like rain on a stick that is fully dry. They seek to promises for refreshment, and find no more savour in them than in the white of an egg; but when the same promises are brought to remembrance by the Spirit the Comforter, who is with them and in them, how full of life and power are they![34]

In addition the Spirit brings consolation by storing up graces to enable believers to cope. Here Owen appeals to Romans 5:3-5. The Spirit pours out God's love into our hearts, and thereby 'sets all our graces to work'.[35]

iii. Even more significantly, the Spirit comes to exercise an ongoing but internal restraint on Christians' lives, and in Owen's quaint phrase, 'drops an awe upon their spirits'[36] to safeguard them against running headlong into sin. The Spirit brings a gladness to obedience, banishing our native sluggishness. Peter is the paradigm here: 'Peter was broken lose and running down hill apace, denying and foreswearing his Master, but Christ restrained him.'[37] This, in turn, becomes for Owen a paradigm of the work of the other comforter, the Holy Spirit, who inwardly 'drops an awe' upon our spirits that causes this holy restraint in order that we may not fall into sin.

A Question of Conscience

Against that background, Owen raises a strategically important question. How do we distinguish between the directions of the Spirit of grace in his guiding and governing of our lives and the delusions of the spirit of the world and of our own sinful heart? How do we distinguish the promptings of the Holy Spirit from the promptings of our own inclinations. He suggests four marks of the leading of the Spirit, by which it is to be contrasted to the instinct of the flesh or the leading of the world.[38]

i. The leading of the Spirit, he says, is regular – in the literal sense: according to the *regulum*: the rule (of Scripture). It is axiomatic for Owen that the Spirit does not work in us to give us a new rule of life, but to bring us light on the rule contained in Scripture and new power to obey its injunctions. In that sense for Owen the fundamental question to ask about guidance will be: Is this course of action consistent with the word of God?

ii. The commands of the Spirit, the directives that the Spirit prompts us to, through the teaching of Scripture, are not grievous (1 John.5: 3). They are in harmony with the word and the word is in harmony with the new creation. To that extent the Christian believer consciously submitted to the word of God will find pleasure in obeying that word, even though there be attendant pain.

iii. The 'motions' or actions of the Spirit, Owen says, are orderly. Just as the covenant of God is ordered in all things and secure (2 Sam. 23:5), so the chief gift of that covenant, the indwelling Spirit, is orderly in the way in which he deals with us. Owen translates this into flesh and blood terms. Here is someone, Owen envisages, who claims frequently that the Holy Spirit is leading them, but whose life is characterised by a deep instability.

> We see some poor souls to be in such bondage as to be hurried up and down, in the matter of duties at the pleasure of Satan. They must run from one to another, and commonly neglect that which they should do.

One can almost see particular members of the congregations Owen pastured in his mind's eyes as he continues:

> When they are at prayer, then they should be at the work of their calling; and when they are at their calling, they are tempted for not laying all aside and running to prayer. Believers know that this is not from the Spirit of God, which makes 'every thing beautiful in its season.'[39]

iv. The 'motions' of the Spirit always tend to glorify God according to his word.

The Spirit, who thus indwells and leads believers, is given as an earnest, a pledge, a down payment on final redemption. This means that the Spirit of Christ is here and now *both* the foretaste of future glory, and *also* an indication of the incompleteness of all present spiritual experience.

This principle is a major clue to Owen's response to the influence of the 'inner light' teaching in his own day (which is not without parallels in our day). He placed great emphasis in his teaching on the struggle of the believer to overcome indwelling sin. In response to antithetical appeals to a supposed liberty of the Spirit which set the Christian free from such low level spirituality, it was enough for Owen to point out that the Spirit, who is the earnest of our inheritance, is the one who causes our groanings: 'We who have the firstfruits of the Spirit groan inwardly as we wait eagerly for the adoption, the redemption of our bodies' (Rom.8: 23). The recognition of this simultaneity of groaning and anticipating stabilises the Christian in the context of misleading teaching.

2. The Sealing of the Spirit

Owen was intensely interested in what Scripture means when it speaks about believers being sealed with the Spirit (Eph. 1:13; 4:30). He was conscious also that the reformed tradition he inherited had not always exegeted Paul's thought here with complete unanimity.[40] Indeed, as late as 1667 Owen wrote about the sealing of the Spirit: 'I am not very clear on the certain particular intendment of this metaphor.'[41]

Here it is worth noting, in parenthesis, that if Owen had the wisdom and courage to say 'I am not completely certain what this text of Scripture means' we should not be slow to share his modesty. Indeed, it is one of the blessings of reformed theology's sense of the incomprehensible greatness of God that it recognises we do not know all of the answers!

In his great work on *Communion with God,* published in 1667, Owen reasoned that it is the promises of God, not the persons who receive them that are in view in the first instance in this sealing: God seals his promises to the believer. And so he concludes that we are sealed when we enjoy a fresh sense of the love of God within us and a comfortable persuasion of acceptance with God. The promises of God – the promises of grace in salvation – are sealed to us and we, correspondingly, enter into the enjoyment of him. The objective produces the subjective.

But in his posthumously published work on the Holy Spirit as Comforter,[42] which emerged from the presses in 1693, ten years after his death, Owen writes, it would seem, more confidently and definitively on the sealing of the Spirit. He notes that,

> The effects of this sealing are gracious operations of the Holy Spirit in and upon believers but the sealing itself is the communication of the Spirit unto us.[43]

The *effects of this sealing* are the gracious operations of the Holy Spirit in the believer; *the sealing itself* is the communication of the Spirit to the believer. Here, conscious of discussions that had taken place, not least among highly-esteemed members of the Puritan Brotherhood (such as Richard Sibbes, John

Preston and Thomas Goodwin who regarded the sealing as 'a second work' of grace giving an immediate assurance of salvation), Owen goes on to note:

> It hath been generally conceived that this sealing of the Spirit is that which gives assurance unto believers and so indeed it doth, although the way whereby it doth hath not been rightly apprehended. And therefore none has been able to declare the especial nature of that act of the Spirit whereby he seals us when such assurance should ensue. But it is indeed not any act of the Spirit in us that is the ground of our assurance but the communication of the Spirit to us.[44]

Here is a wise and mature man dealing sensitively with a difficult theological and pastoral issue. His basic distinction is clear enough. He is saying the sealing of the Spirit does indeed bring assurance, but the sealing of the Spirit is not to be thought of as a specific act of the Spirit, so much as the act of the communication of the Spirit to us. In essence, for Owen the Spirit himself is the seal. In that context – and here we come near to the entry point to our discussion – he moves back to the basic principle that the Lord Jesus Christ is the one whom the Father sealed (John 6: 27). This can only mean that the Father communicated the Spirit to him without measure. What was true of Christ then, *mutatis mutandis*, becomes true of believers.

Clearly in this context Owen is anxious not to diminish the role of the Spirit in giving a powerful assurance of salvation in Jesus Christ through the ministry of the Spirit. He is simply making the exegetical point that this is not the precise meaning of the Scriptures to which appeal is made. Rather the Spirit is himself the seal. As he ministers, assurance of grace and salvation follow. The testimony of the Spirit, to put it in these terms, is an effect of the presence of the Spirit as seal and activates the believer's sense of assurance.

Owen provides a vivid and colourful word-picture of this in his exposition of communion with God. While it is nuanced in a distinctively Owenian way, his thinking is characteristic of many of his Puritan brethren:

> The soul, by the power of its own conscience, is brought before the law of God. There a man puts in his plea, – that he is a child of God, that he belongs to God's family; and for this end produceth all his evidences, every thing whereby faith gives him an interest in God.

The issue is clear: Is this man a believer? He responds: 'I am a believer. Here is the basis of my conviction that I belong to God's family; here are the evidences. These are the things that faith has wrought.' But, says Owen,

> Satan, in the meantime, opposeth with all his might; sin and law assist him; many flaws are found his in his evidences; the truth of them all is questioned; and the soul hangs in suspense as to the issue. In the midst of the plea and contest, the Comforter comes, and, by a word of promise, or otherwise, overpowers the heart with a comfortable persuasion (and bears down all objections) that his plea is good, and that he is a child of God ... When our spirits are pleading their right and title, he comes in and bears witness on our side.
>
> When the Lord Jesus Christ at one word stilled the raging of the sea and wind, all that were with him knew there was divine power at hand, Matt viii. 25–27. And when the Holy Ghost by one word stills the tumults and storms that are raised in the soul, giving it an immediate calm and security, it knows his divine power, and rejoices in his presence.[45]

In a word, Owen is saying the Spirit does for us as seal what Christ did for the disciples as Saviour.

This final reference to Matthew 8: 25–27 is particularly telling and poignant to those who are familiar with the biography of John Owen. Here, for a moment, in this magisterial work of rich trinitarian theology, like a great artist he paints himself into a small corner of his own masterwork. For it was through a sermon on this text, preached by an unknown substitute for the great Edmund Calamy (whom the young Owen had hoped to hear), that his years of spiritual struggle were brought to an end. He had then emerged from the grey areas of uncertainty to a deep and lasting assurance. Here, as it were, is the theological formulation of the reality Owen had experienced in a memorably personal way.

It is fitting for us to conclude our brief consideration of Owen's teaching on the Holy Spirit on this note. In that life-defining experience the knowledge of the truth had become the knowledge of the power of the truth.

In summary, then, the ministry of the Spirit will always affect believers in these three ways:

i. Since the Holy Spirit is the third Person of the Godhead, the one who proceeds from the Father and the Son, the Eternal Spirit, he is to be worshipped, loved and adored.

Owen well understood that the Holy Spirit, in relationship to Christ, does not bring glory to himself but to the Son. But the Spirit's commitment to bring glory to the Son does not justify our failure to give glory to the Spirit as well as to the Son. The role of the Spirit within the Trinitarian economy does not minimise his full deity, nor does it exempt us from admiration, adoration, praise and devotion to the one who so lovingly shines on the Son and comes to believers as the Spirit of grace. Here Owen's trinitarianism needs to be recovered. And this means learning to worship, as well as to engage in fellowship with, the Holy Spirit.

ii. The Holy Spirit's work is to reproduce in us the holiness of Christ. We must therefore never resist him in this ministry. Rather, as Owen expounds in detail in his great work on the mortification of sin,[46] by the power of the Spirit we are to put to death all that remains in us that is alien to our Lord.

iii. If as the *Eternal* Spirit he is to be worshipped, and as the *Holy* Spirit he reproduces the holiness of Christ, then as the *indwelling* Spirit he is not to be grieved (Eph.4: 30). To grieve someone, says Owen, is to display the unkindness of unrequited love. In the case of the Spirit it is the 'defect of an answerable love unto the fruits and testimonies of his love which we have received.'[47]

To grieve the Holy Spirit is by our lives to disappoint him who has loved us with an eternal love. And so Owen pleads with us: We are the recipients of signal mercies, will we not return to him the holy love he seeks from our hearts; the full obedience he seeks to work in our lives?

Such grieving of the Holy Spirit, Owen believes, is heightened precisely because of the intimacy of the Spirit with the Son and the intimacy of the Spirit with the believer. He who dwells in us loves our Saviour; he who dwells in us loves us, because Christ is our Saviour. Those who love us most are most grieved by us when we fail. So it is, says Owen, with the Spirit.

Or to use the words of a greater even than Owen, 'Do not grieve the Holy Spirit by whom you were sealed for the day of redemption' (Eph.4: 30).

Notes

[1] *The Works of John Owen*, ed. W.H. Goold, Edinburgh 1850-53, vols 3 and 4

[2] Edmund Campion (1540-1581), along with Robert Parsons (1546-1610) came to England from the Continent in 1580 to spearhead the Jesuit English Mission. Campion was arrested and executed at Tyburn in 1581.

[3] *De Justificatione* III.2.3. Cardinal Robert Bellarmine (1542-1621) was a Jesuit scholar and personal theologian to the pope. He was canonized in 1930 and made a Doctor of the Church. He is the Counter Reformation theologian most frequently cited by the Puritans and regarded universally by them as the most formidable. The Council of Trent's Decree on Justification (Session VI, chapter 9) implies a similar perspective.

[4] *Works*, 3.7

[5] Owen's familiarity with the work on the Holy Spirit of e.g., Cyprian (c200-258), Didymus the Blind (c309-398), Basil the Great (329-379), Ambrose (339-397), Chrysostom (c344-407) and others is evident in the course of his exposition.

[6] See, e.g. his *Contre la secte phantastique et furieuse des Libertins qui se nomment Spirituelz* published in 1545, trs and ed. B.W. Farley in *John Calvin;Ttreatises Against the Anabaptists and Against the Libertines*, Grand Rapids, 1982, pp.161-326.

[7] *Works* 3.192

[8] See e.g. *Works* 1. XXV-XXVI, XXIX-XXX

[9] David Clarkson (1622-1686), Fellow of Clare Hall, Cambridge 1645-1651, and then until the Great Ejection in 1662 curate of Mortlake, Surrey. He became colleague to the then-ailing Owen in 1682 and succeeded him in ministry until his own death.

[10] The whole sermon, published in 1720, is reprinted in William Orme, *Memoirs of the Life and Writings of John Owen*, in *The Works of John Owen,* ed. T. Russell, 1826, volume 1.

[11] See the comments of H.N. Ridderbos, *Paul an Outline of his Theology*, trs. J.R. de Witt, Eerdmans, Grand Rapids, 1975, p.14ff.

[12] e.g. *Works* III.162

[13] *Works* 3. 162-164

[14] It is significant that the chapter title Owen chooses in this context speaks of the 'work of the Holy Spirit with respect unto the head of the new creation.' The Last Adam Christology is of considerable significance in the pattern of his thought.

[15] *Works* 3.169. The entire section is important for Owen's Christology as well as his Pneumatology.

[16] *Works* 3.169-70

[17] *Works* 3.170

[18] *Works* 3. 170-171

[19] *Works* 3.174

[20] *Works* 23.307

[21] *Works* 3.178

[22] *Works* 3.176-77

[23] *Works* 3.180-81. The whole passage is remarkable for its meditative tenderness.

[24] *Works* 3.181-83

[25] *Works* 3.182

[26] *Works* 3.185

[27] Owen deals with these themes throughout *Works* 3 and 4.

[28] *Works* 3.337-366

[29] *Works* 4.383

[30] *Works* 11.333

[31] He does, of course, provide this comfort to believers 'at all times, and on all occasions wherein they really stand in need of spiritual consolation.' *Works* 4.379

[32] *Works* 11.342-346

[33] *Works* 11.346-348

[34] *Works* 11.347

[35] *Works* 11.348

[36] *Works* 11.349

[37] *Ibid.*

[38] For what follows see *Works* 11.363-4.

[39] *Works* 11.364

[40] For further discussion see S.B. Ferguson, *John Owen on the Christian Life*, Edinburgh 1987,pp. 116-124.

[41] *Works* 2.242

[42] *Works* 4.353-419

[43] *Works* 4.400. Emphasis mine.
[44] *Works* 4. 405. Cf his earlier comments pp.400-401.
[45] *Works* 2:241-2
[46] *Works,* 6.1-86
[47] *Works,* 4.414

Chapter Five

'The one and Only, absolute and perfect, rule':

JOHN OWEN AND THE CHALLENGE OF THE QUAKERS

Michael Haykin is presently Professor of Church History at Heritage Baptist College and Heritage Theological Seminary in Cambridge, Ontario. He has published works on the doctrine of the Holy Spirit in the Patristic Period and on English Dissent.

We persuade men to take the Scriptures as the only rule, and the holy promised Spirit of God, sought by ardent prayers and supplications, in the use of all means appointed by Christ for that end, for their guide. They deal with men to turn themselves into themselves, and to attend unto the light within them...

Works IV, 159-160

JOHN OWEN AND THE CHALLENGE OF THE QUAKERS

In June of 1654, Elizabeth Fletcher (c.1638-1658) and Elizabeth Leavens (d.1665), two Quakers from Kendal, Westmoreland, visited Oxford, the first to bring the Quaker message to the university town.[1] They sought to warn the students there about the ungodly nature of academia and convince them that their real need was not intellectual illumination but the inner light given by the Holy Spirit. Their message, though, fell largely on deaf ears. Elizabeth Fletcher felt led by God to resort to a more dramatic testimony to arrest the students' attention. She stripped off her clothing and walked semi-naked through the streets of Oxford as 'a signe against the Hippocriticall profession they then made there, being then Presbetereans & Independants, which profession she told them the Lord would strip them of, so that their Nakedness should appear'.[2] Fletcher's 'going naked as a sign', a practice not uncommon among the early Quakers,[3] sparked a hostile reaction among the students. Some of students seized her and her companion, dragged them through a miry ditch and then half-drowned them under the water-pump on the grounds of St John's College. At some point Fletcher was also either thrown over a gravestone or pushed into an open grave, sustaining injuries that plagued her for the rest of her short life.

It appears, though, that this ordeal did little to dampen the spirits of the two women. The following Sunday they visited an Oxford church where they interrupted the service in order to give a divine warning to the congregation. This time they were arrested and imprisoned in the Bocardo prison. The following day, John Owen, who, as University Vice-Chancellor was responsible for discipline within the University, accused the two Quakers of blaspheming the Holy Spirit and profaning the Scriptures. Convinced that if the women's behaviour were left unpunished it would incite disorder in the University, he ordered the women to be whipped and expelled from the town.

Two years later Owen had another memorable encounter with the Quakers. This time it was a theological debate in Whitehall Palace with the man who would come to be viewed as the foremost figure in the seventeenth-century British Quaker community, George Fox (1624-1691).[4] Fox later recounted what transpired when he and another Quaker, Edward Pyott (d.1670), visited Oliver Cromwell (1599-1658), who was then ruling England as Lord Protector.

Edward Pyott and I went to Whitehall after a time and when we came before him [i.e. Cromwell] there was one Dr. John Owen, Vice-Chancellor of Oxford with him: so we was moved to speak to Oliver Cromwell concerning the sufferings of Friends and laid them before him and turned him to the light of Christ who had enlightened every man that cometh into the world: and he said it was a natural light and we showed him the contrary and how it was divine and spiritual from Christ the spiritual and heavenly man, which was called the life in Christ, the Word and the light in us. And the power of the Lord God riz in me, and I was moved to bid him lay down his crown at the feet of Jesus. Several times I spoke to him to the same effect, and I was standing by the table; and he came and sat upon the table's side by me and said

> he would be as high as I was. And so he continued speak-
> ing against the light of Christ Jesus...[5]

These two incidents display some of the central features of early Quakerism: its emphasis on the divine light within every human being (a conviction drawn from John 1:9), its fiery pros-elytizing, its contempt of university learning, and its reliance on dramatic and socially disruptive gestures.

I. Quakerism during the Commonwealth

The Quaker movement was a product of the turmoil of the English Civil War (1642-1651), when familiar social, political, and religious boundaries were being swept away by the tide of conflict and when tried and true religious practices and beliefs no longer seemed to carry any weight. Numerous individuals, many of them raised in a Puritan environment with its empha-sis on radical depravity and the need for the sovereign, con-verting work of the Spirit, had begun seeking for a God who would bring peace to their souls in the midst of the massive upheaval of the times. Some of these so-called 'Seekers' longed for a restoration of the charismatic vitality and simplicity they believed to be characteristic of the Apostolic Church. As J. F. McGregor points out, they regarded the sign of a true church of Christ to be 'its possession of the grace given to the apostles and demonstrated through miracles'. Since none of the Puri-tan congregations claimed to be in possession of such charis-matic gifts, the Seekers felt that they had to withdraw from them and wait for what they hoped would be a new divine dispensa-tion.[6] For many Seekers, that divine dispensation appeared with the advent of the Quakers and their message.

Although there were a number of key figures in Quakerism's early days, men such as Edward Burrough (1634-1662), Richard

Hubberthorne (1628-1662), William Dewsbury (1621-1688), and James Nayler (*c.*1618-1660), it was George Fox who served as the principal catalyst to bring together many of these Seekers into 'a loose kind of church fellowship with a coherent ideology'.[7] By the late 1660s most of these early Quaker leaders were dead, and Fox survived to become the nucleus around which the Quaker community eventually coalesced in the late seventeenth century. A one-time shepherd and shoemaker, 'literate, but not learned',[8] Fox left his native village of Drayton-in-the-Clay (now Fenny Drayton), Leicestershire, in 1643 and for lengthy periods of time over the next four years tramped through the Midlands and as far south as London. His goal during this period of physical wandering seems to have been the acquisition of spiritual wisdom. He spent a considerable amount of time with the General (i.e. Arminian) Baptists, whose influence on him may be seen in his later rejection of orthodox Puritan soteriology, in particular, the doctrine of predestination.[9]

Finally, in 1647 and 1648 Fox found wisdom 'without', he wrote, 'the help of any man, book or writing'.[10] Through a series of what he called 'openings', experiences of inner enlightenment, he became convinced, among other things, 'that being bred at Oxford or Cambridge was not enough to fit and qualify men to be ministers of Christ',[11] and that genuine Christianity was essentially a matter of inward spiritual experience. 'The Lord God,' Fox later recalled in his *Journal*,

opened to me by his invisible power how that every man was enlightened by the divine light of Christ; and I saw it shine through all, and that they, that believed in it came out of condemnation and came to the light of life and became the children of it, but they that hated it, and did not believe in it, were condemned by it, though they made a profession of Christ. This I saw in the pure openings of the Light without the help of any man,

neither did I then know, where to find it in the Scriptures; though afterwards, searching the Scriptures, I
found it. For I saw in that Light and Spirit which was
before Scripture was given forth, and which led the holy
men of God to give them forth, that all must come to
that Spirit, if they would know God, or Christ, or the
Scriptures aright, which they that gave them forth were
led and taught by.[12]

John 1:9 ('that was the true Light, which lighteth every man
that cometh into the world'), to which Fox alludes in the earlier
part of this passage, was at the core of Fox's distinctive
message and that of his fellow Quakers. They understood this
text to teach that every individual was born with the light of
Christ, which, though darkened by sin, was never fully extinguished. For those who became convinced by the Quaker
message, this light had succeeded in breaking through the
barrier of sin to unite their souls with Christ.[13] This verse thus
described what they knew 'experimentally', to use Fox's own
description of his spiritual illumination. Moreover, this light of
Christ shone within their dark hearts, they believed, independent
of the various means of grace normally stressed by the
Puritans, means such as the reading of the Scriptures.

This text also helped define the Quaker mission. After his
conversion, for instance, Fox was conscious of being
commanded 'to turn people to that inward light, spirit and grace,
by which all might know their salvation, and their way to God;
even that divine spirit, which would lead them into all Truth,
and which I infallibly knew would never deceive any.'[14] We 'call
All men to look to the Light within their own consciences,'
another Quaker convert, Samuel Fisher (1605-1665), who had
been a General Baptist, declared of the goal of Quaker
proselytizing. 'By the leadings of that Light,' he continued, 'they
may come to God, and work out their Salvation.'[15]

In the first decade of the Quaker movement, this message enjoyed phenomenal success. 1652 is often regarded by historians as the start of Quakerism.[16] It was during the spring of that year Fox took his message north to the Pennines and Westmoreland. On Whitsunday that year, Fox preached to a large gathering of a thousand Seekers not far from Kendal. 'As soon as I heard him declare ... that the Light of Christ in man was the way to Christ,' recalled Francis Howgill (1618-1669), a local preacher and one-time Baptist, 'I believed the eternal word of truth, and that of God in my conscience sealed to it.' Not only was he convinced of the truth of Fox's message, but, he remembered, so were 'many hundred more, who thirsted after the Lord'.[17]

The Quaker message took deep root in northern England, in particular, in the counties of Westmoreland, Lancashire, Yorkshire, and Cumberland. Over the next decade it spread south and had a profound impact on at least four other areas: Cheshire; London and those counties directly to the north and east of the capital (Hertfordshire, Buckinghamshire, Cambridgeshire and Essex); the town of Bristol, along with Somerset and Wiltshire; and the Midlands counties of Warwickshire and Worcestershire.[18] Quaker missionary endeavours were not confined to the British Isles, however. By 1660 zealous Quaker evangelists had gone as far afield as Massachusetts, Germany, Rome, Malta, and Jerusalem.[19] As a result of these endeavours, it is estimated that there were at least between 35,000 and 40,000 Quakers in Britain alone by the early 1660s. According to Barry Reay, there may have been as many as 60,000.[20]

II. Quaker versus Puritan

Alongside the Quaker emphasis on the illumination that came from the light within, which the Quakers variously called the indwelling Christ or indwelling Spirit,[21] there was, as Richard Bauman has noted, the vigorous assertion that Quaker experience involved hearing a divine inner voice. The Quakers did not deny that God could and did speak to people mediately through the written text of Scripture, but they were convinced that they also knew and enjoyed the Spirit's immediate inspiration and guidance like the Apostles and saints of the New Testament era.[22] In the words of the Quaker theologian William Penn (1644-1718), immediate experiences of the Spirit 'once were the great Foundation of both their [i.e. New Testament believers] Knowledge and Comfort, though now mockt at ... with great Derision in a Quaker'.[23] In Bauman's words, 'direct personal communion with God speaking within was the core religious experience of early Quakerism'.[24]

Bauman's comment is well borne out by a letter that Isaac Penington the Younger (1616-1679) wrote to a fellow Quaker, Nathanael Stonar, in 1670. Penington, who is 'a prime example of the intellectual sophistication' of a number of early Quaker converts,[25] told his correspondent that one of the main differences between themselves and other 'professors', by whom he meant Congregationalists and Baptists, was 'concerning *the rule'*. While the latter asserted that the Scriptures were the rule by which men and women ought to direct their lives and thinking, Penington was convinced that the indwelling Spirit of life is 'nearer and more powerful, than the words, or outward relations concerning those things in the Scriptures'. As Penington noted:

> The Lord, in the gospel state, hath promised to be present with his people; not as a wayfaring man, for a night, but to *dwell in them and walk in them.* Yea, if they be tempted and in danger of erring, they shall hear a voice behind them, saying, 'This is the way, walk in it.' Will they not grant this to be a rule, as well as the

Scriptures? Nay, is not this a more full direction to the heart, in that state, than it can pick to itself out of the Scriptures? ...the Spirit, which gave forth the words, is greater than the words; therefore we cannot but prize Him himself, and set Him higher in our heart and thoughts, than the words which testify of Him, though they also are very sweet and precious to our taste.[26]

Penington here affirms that the Quakers esteemed the Scriptures as 'sweet and precious', but he was equally adamant that the indwelling Spirit was to be regarded as the supreme authority when it came to direction for Christian living and thinking.[27]

Similarly George Fox, listening to a sermon on 2 Peter 1:19, in which the preacher told the congregation 'that the Scriptures were the touchstone and judge by which they were to try all doctrines, religions, and opinions', found himself unable to contain his disagreement. He cried out, 'Oh no, it is not the Scriptures.' He then proceeded to tell what presumably was a shocked audience that the touchstone and judge was 'the Holy Spirit, by which the holy men of God gave forth the Scriptures, whereby opinions, religions, and judgements were to be tried; for it led into all Truth, and so gave the knowledge of the Truth'.[28] And when some Baptists in Huntingdonshire and Cambridgeshire became Quakers they were quick to assert that henceforth the 'light in their consciences was the rule they desire to walk by', not the Scriptures.[29]

Quakerism thus tended to exalt the Spirit at the expense of the Word.[30] And on not a few occasions this led the early Quakers into quite bizarre patterns of behaviour and speech. Elizabeth Fletcher's going naked for a sign is but one example.[31] Others would include Margaret Fell (1614-1702), Fox's future wife, describing Fox as 'the fountain of eternal life' to whom 'all nations shall bow',[32] the acclamation made by Richard Sale (d.1658) to Fox, 'Praises, praises, eternal praises to thee forevermore, who was and is and is to come, who is god over all, blessed forever,'[33] and James Nayler's shocking re-enactment of Christ's ride into Jerusalem at Bristol in 1656.[34] It was this willingness on the part of the Quakers to appear to go 'behind and beyond' the Scriptures that explains much of the 'unmitigated abhorrence' for them that one finds in Puritan writings of the time.[35]

We turn then to look at one of Puritanism's sharpest critics of the Quakers, namely, John Owen. Unlike some of his Puritan contemporaries, though, his critique is informed not primarily 'by vituperation, but by close and careful argument'.[36]

III. John Owen, critic of the Quakers

Owen is quite prepared to admit that some 'edification' can be found in the 'silent [worship] meetings' of the Quakers.[37] On the whole, however, he sees them as 'poor deluded souls'.[38] Their teaching about the inner light is an attack on the work and person of the Holy Spirit, a 'pretended light', and possibly even 'a dark product of Satan'.[39] When they pointed to the trembling and quaking that sometimes gripped men and women in their meetings as evidence of the Spirit's powerful presence, Owen saw only 'a spirit of bondage' that threw them 'into an un-son-like frame'.[40] Their worship is further flawed by their discarding of the 'sacraments, ... baptism and the supper of the Lord, which are so great a part of the mystical worship of the church'. Owen is not surprised, though. Both of these ordinances speak about the heart of the Christian faith, 'The sanctifying and justifying blood of Christ.' But the Quakers, Owen is convinced, have forsaken the gospel's emphasis on the objective, atoning work of Christ for a focus upon the 'light within men', and these two ordinances cannot 'contribute any thing to the furtherance, increase, or establishment, of that light'.[41] At the heart of this erroneous focus of the Quakers, Owen felt, was their failure to grasp the Trinitarian nature of the work of redemption. 'Convince any of them of the doctrine of the Trinity,' he wrote in 1674, 'and all the rest of their imaginations vanish into smoke.'[42]

Owen argues that the Quaker lauding of the light within, which they often identified with the Spirit, seems to be a subtle exaltation of the Spirit by the Spirit. Jesus' statement in John 16:14 – 'he [i.e. the Spirit] shall glorify me; for he shall receive of mine, and shall show it to you' – is crucial to understanding the salvific work of the Trinity, and it reveals that the message of the Quakers is actually an inversion of 'The order of the divine dispensations.' The Holy Spirit has not come to glorify himself. According to Owen's reading of John 16:14, the Father sent the Spirit in love to make the Son 'glorious, honourable, and of high esteem in the hearts of believers' and to shed 'abroad the love of God in our hearts'. The Spirit's mission in this regard runs parallel, as it were, to the Son's being sent by the Father 'to suffer at Jerusalem … for us' and bring glory to the one who sent him.[43]

Owen's most concentrated attack on the Quakers is found in his *Pro Sacris Scripturis Exercitationes adversus Fanaticos*, which was published in 1659.[44] In his biography of the Congregationalist theologian, Peter Toon suggests that the writing of the treatise in Latin is a deliberate affirmation of traditional learning in the face of the Quakers' denigration of university education.[45] Toon may well be right, for Owen devotes a substantial portion of the second chapter of this treatise to a defence of sound exegesis and exegetical techniques, many of which would be learned in the university environment of the theological college.[46]

The treatise is divided into four chapters. In the first, Owen refutes the claim of the Quakers that the Scriptures should not be termed 'The Word of God,' since, they argued, this title properly belongs to Christ alone.[47] Owen, of course, knows that there are biblical texts which do call Christ 'The Word,' passages such as Revelation 19:13, John 1:1 and John 1:14. Owen can thus agree with the Quakers: 'Christ Himself is the Word of God, the essential Word.'[48] Yet, this term is frequently used by the Bible as a self-description, as Owen easily shows. He cites Mark 7:13, for example, where Jesus accuses the Pharisees of preferring their traditions to the commands of the Old Testament and so 'making the Word of God of no effect'. The Scriptures are also to be considered a spoken declaration of the will and mind of God and, as such, his Word. Owen then points his readers to verses like Exodus 34:1 and Revelation 21:5, which refer to this inscripturation of God's speaking. He also notes a passage like Colossians 3:16, which mentions 'The Word of Christ,' which, he rightly states, cannot be Christ himself. 'Scripture,' he concludes, 'is God's written Word, speaking of him to us.'[49]

Owen's quarrel with the Quakers over the use of this phrase 'Word of God' is no mere issue of semantics. As he would later write in his 1678 treatise *The Causes, Ways, and Means of Understanding the Mind of God as Revealed in his Word*:

> Our belief of the Scriptures to be the word of God, or a divine revelation, and our understanding of the mind and will of God as revealed in them, are the *two springs* of all our interest in Christian religion. From them are all those streams of light and truth derived whereby our souls are watered, refreshed, and made fruitful unto God.[50]

The second chapter of *Pro Sacris Scripturis* opens with what initially appears to be an extraneous issue – a refutation of the claim of the Roman Catholic magisterium to be 'the one, perfect, independent, visible judge and expositor' of Scripture.[51] The

link between the Roman Catholic view of the Scriptures and
that of the Quakers in Owen's mind seems to be that both groups
effectively undermined the authority of God's Word.[52] Roman
Catholics of that day rejected its sufficiency, while the Quakers
denied its necessity. There is an area, though, where Owen is in
agreement with seventeenth-century Roman Catholic thought:
proper public interpreters of God's Word are necessary.

Among the English Puritans, however, the question of who
could publicly expound the Word of God had been a hotly
debated one.[53] Those who were more conservative, like Richard
Baxter (1615-1691), insisted that ordination was the regular
pathway to preaching. Owen disagreed.

> Let a faithful man ... being furnished with the knowledge
> of God and the requisite Spiritual gifts for the edification
> of others (graciously bestowed upon him by God), and
> also having the time and other things necessary for the
> right performance of this duty granted him by
> providence, then I certainly would allow him to interpret
> the Scriptures and to meet with others for their
> edification, even though he does not intend ever to holy
> orders – providing only that he makes no interruption
> of an established ministry. ...Where Christ has provided
> the gifts there *must* be a vocation.[54]

Owen's insistence that lay preaching not be an 'interruption of
an established ministry' is an important point in this statement.
It indicates his opposition to those radicals, like the Quakers,
who wanted to go even further and secure the complete freedom
of the pulpit for anyone who wanted to express his opinions.[55]

Having demonstrated the necessity of fit expositors of God's
Word, Owen can now tackle the Quaker dislike of exposition
and expository techniques as well as their rejection of the use
of commentaries and other books to ascertain the meaning of
the Scriptures. God's gift of human reason, which sets humanity

apart from animals, and the necessity of Scripture knowledge so as to be instructed in the ways of God require these very things the Quakers despise.[56] 'God, in his infinite wisdom, not only arranged the declaration of his will in the Scripture,' Owen remarks, 'but also arranged that declaration in such a manner as absolutely necessitates the duty of exposition as a function of the Church as long as the Scriptures shall last.'[57]

Chapter Three deals with the 'perfection' of the Scriptures. From personal conversation with Quakers and perusal of some of their books,[58] Owen lists a number of major Quaker opinions with regard to the Scriptures that he wishes to refute. Two in particular receive detailed attention in Owen's rebuttal. Owen notes their denial that 'The Scriptures are the settled, ordinary, perfect and unshakable rule for divine worship and human obedience.' They also argued, he records, that the goal of the Scriptures is to bring men and women to heed the 'inner light' within them, and once that has been achieved, the Bible's main purpose has been fulfilled.[59]

Owen's refutation of the first of these convictions begins by stressing that the Scriptures were given to fulfill two broad purposes. In line with his Reformed heritage, Owen reasons that the ultimate purpose of Scripture is doxological, namely, the glory of God. 'Since God does all that he does for his own sake and for his own glory, and as he has produced this surpassing achievement of the written Scripture, given by his absolute sovereign will, then he can have given it for no less supreme purpose.' A secondary purpose of the Scriptures is soteriological. It has been given for the salvation of sinners, 'the instructing of men in the knowledge and worship of God'. Owen insists that these two purposes dovetail, for it is as men and women are brought by the instruction of Scripture to salvation that God's glory is secured. Since Scripture perfectly achieves that for which it has been given, it must be deemed 'the one and only, absolute and perfect, rule for the whole of divine worship and obedience.'[60] A catena of Bible verses is given as support.

> [Scripture's] purpose ... is to engender faith. 'These
> things have been written, that ye might believe' (John
> 20:31); 'Faith cometh by hearing, and hearing by the
> word of God' (Romans 10:17). It is 'the certainty of those
> things' (Luke 1:4) which is able 'to make thee wise unto
> salvation' (2 Timothy 3:15); 'a sure word of prophecy'
> (2 Peter 1:19), through which we may be 'thoroughly
> furnished unto all good works' (2 Timothy 3:17), and it
> is by it that we gain life eternal (John 5:39, 20:31)...
> 'The law of the Lord is perfect, converting the soul'
> (Psalm 19:7), and so it is 'a lamp unto my feet, and a
> light unto my path' (Psalm 119:105), it is 'the power of
> God unto salvation' (Romans 1:16), that which is 'able
> to make thee wise unto salvation' (2 Timothy 3:15) and
> 'thoroughly furnished unto all good works' (verse 17). It
> is that which 'is able to save your souls' (James 1:21).
> So Scripture accomplishes all things which are neces-
> sary for God's glory and man's salvation.[61]

Other arguments for Scripture's perfection are drawn from biblical texts that condemn adding to the Scriptures and from the frequency of God's command in his Word that his people diligently heed the Scriptures. Owen also adduces the work of deception carried on by Satan, who has used the 'mask of pretended revelations and interior inspiration' throughout history to ensnare human beings. In order to provide 'a constant aid and guide' to embattled humanity, God thus caused his Word to be carefully inscripturated.[62]

Refutation of the other major Quaker argument, namely, their doctrine of the 'inner light', is deemed by Owen to be so important that he devotes the fourth and final chapter of his work to this subject.

IV. The inner light and John 1:9

Owen initially sets his reply to the Quaker doctrine of the inner light within the context of a discussion of two central aspects of the history of salvation. First, there is the fact of the Fall, an event that extinguished the 'inborn spiritual light' which Adam and Eve possessed in the paradisal state. There was, in Owen's words, an 'actual inrush of spiritual shade' when they fell, and they, as did their progeny, henceforth lived and walked in darkness. This situation did not essentially change until the coming of Christ, though the darkness of humanity was alleviated to some degree by the light cast by the Old Testament prophets. It was the coming of Christ, the true light of the entire world, and the outpouring of his Spirit that brought sight to the spiritually blind and so transformed 'his people from the domain of darkness into the glory of his most marvelous light'.[63] Owen's point in reciting these facts is to stress that any remnant of Adamic light which remains in human nature has power enough only to reveal that all human beings are 'by nature dead, blind, deaf, darkened of intellect, nay, are very blindness and darkness itself'. To effect salvation, though, that requires 'the infusion of an outside and spiritual light to irradiate hearts and minds'.[64]

Owen rightly understands the Quaker concept of the inner light to be an assertion that the Fall was not as radical an event as Reformed theology maintained and thus that the 'inborn spiritual light' possessed prior to the Fall could still give a saving knowledge of God.[65] Although Owen was prepared to admit that this light could attain to some valid knowledge about God,[66] he essentially rejected the Quaker position. As he stated a number of years later in his *ΧΡΙΣΤΟΛΟΓΙΑ: or, a Declaration of the Glorious Mystery of the Person of Christ God and Man* (1679), when he had occasion to comment on the best of Greek philosophical thought:

> There was a notion, even among the philosophers, that the principal endeavour of a wise man was to be like unto God. But in the improvement of it, the best of them fell into foolish and proud imaginations. Howbeit, the notion itself was the principal beam of our *primigenial light*, the last relic of our natural perfections ... But those persons who had nothing but the absolute essential properties of the divine nature to contemplate on in the light of reason, failed all of them, both in the notion itself of conformity unto God, and especially in the practical improvement of it.[67]

The lie is also given to the Quaker notion of the inner light being a common possession of all men by what Scripture tells us about the gift of the Spirit, which the Quakers often equated with the inner light. Owen notes that a passage like Jude 19 declares that 'the Spirit of Christ is expressly *not* possessed by some.' And referring to Romans 8:9b ('if any man have not the Spirit of Christ, he is none of his'), Owen deduces that 'Christ does not bestow his Holy Spirit ... on all and sundry.'[68]

Not surprisingly Owen devotes some space to the exegesis of John 1:9 – 'that was the true Light, which lighteth every man that cometh (εφρχοωμεου) into the world' – the textual linch-pin of the Quaker position.[69] The Quaker reading of this verse assumed that the participle 'coming' referred back to 'every man'. Owen's exposition of this text, on the other hand, is informed by his remarks earlier in the chapter about the history of salvation. Christ, the true light, by means of his incarnation gives light to sinners who are sitting 'shrouded in deep shadow'. Thus Owen states: 'It is not said that Christ illuminates *every* man coming into the world, but rather that he, coming into the world, illuminates every man.' In other words, Owen understands the referent of the participle 'coming' to be the 'true Light'.

Owen's interpretation means that the illumination about which the Johannine text speaks is spiritual, not a natural one of which all human beings partake. In Owen's words, it is 'a fruit of renewal by grace, rather than infusion by creation'. As Owen further recognizes, his reading of the passage commits him to taking 'every man' in a relative sense, as meaning 'all of God's people', and not in an absolute sense, as 'all people without exception'.[70]

The means by which this saving enlightenment comes Owen asserts to be 'The Word and the Spirit.'[71] To use terms from his later treatise *ΧΡΙΣΤΟΛΟΓΙΑ*, the Word, is the *medium revelans* or *lumen deferens*, the objective light by which knowledge of Christ is conveyed to our minds. Without the Scriptures we can see nothing of Christ. The Spirit, on the other hand, is the *lumen præparans, elevans, disponens subjectum*, the light that illuminates the mind by means of the Scriptures to spiritually 'Behold and discern the glory of God in the face of Christ.'[72] Quaker assertions of the inner light and their apparent devaluing of the Scriptures thus cut the nerve of true vital experience of the saving light of Christ. Nearly twenty years later, Owen would sum up the difference between those of his persuasion and the Quakers along these very lines:

> We persuade men to take the Scripture as the *only rule*, and the holy promised Spirit of God, sought by ardent prayers and supplications, in the use of all means appointed by Christ for that end, *for their guide*. They deal with men to turn into themselves, and to attend unto the light within them. Whilst we build on these most distant principles, the difference between us is irreconcilable, and will be eternal. …Until, therefore, they return unto 'the law and testimony', – without which, whatsoever is pretended, there is no *light* in any, – we have no more to do but, labouring to preserve the flock of Christ in the profession of the 'faith once delivered unto the saints,, to commit the difference between the *word and Spirit* on the one hand, and the *light within* on the other, unto the decision of Jesus Christ at the last day.[73]

Notes

[1] For brief biographical sketches of these two women, see R. L. Greaves, 'Fletcher, Elizabeth' in his and Robert Zaller, eds., *Biographical Dictionary of British Radicals in the Seventeenth Century* (Brighton, Sussex: Harvester Press, 1982), I, 292 and D. P. Ludlow, 'Leavens, Elizabeth' in R. L. Greaves and Robert Zaller, eds., *Biographical Dictionary of British Radicals in the Seventeenth Century* (Brighton, Sussex: Harvester Press, 1983), II, 182. For the following account of their visit to Oxford, see William Sewel, *The History of the Rise, Increase and Progress of the Christian People Called Quakers* (New York: Baker & Crane, 1844), I, 120-121, and Peter Toon, *God's Statesman: The Life and Work of John Owen: Pastor, Educator, Theologian* (Exeter: Paternoster Press, 1971), 76. For a similar account of the entrance of Quakerism into Cambridge University, see John Twigg, *The University of Cambridge and the English Revolution 1625-1688* (Woodbridge, Suffolk: Boydell Press/Cambridge: Cambridge University Press, 1990), 193-195.

[2] Kenneth L. Carroll, 'Early Quakers and Going Naked as a Sign', *Quaker History*, 67 (1978), 80.

[3] For two excellent studies of this phenomenon, see *ibid.*, 69-87, and Richard Bauman, *Let Your Words Be Few: Symbolism of Speaking and Silence among Seventeenth-Century Quakers* (Cambridge: Cambridge University Press, 1983), 84-94. See also the related studies by Kenneth L. Carroll, 'Sackcloth and Ashes and other Signs and Wonders', *The Journal of the Friends' Historical Society*, 53 (1972-1975), 314-325 and *idem*, 'Quaker Attitudes towards Sign and Wonders', *The Journal of the Friends' Historical Society*, 54 (1976-1982), 70-84.

[4] For a recent biography of Fox, see H. Larry Ingle, *First Among Friends: George Fox and the Creation of Quakerism* (New York/Oxford: Oxford University Press, 1994).

[5] *The Journal of George Fox*, ed. John L. Nickalls (Philadelphia: Religious Society of Friends, 1985), 274-275.

[6] J. F. McGregor, 'Seekers and Ranters' in his and B. Reay, eds., *Radical Religion in the English Revolution* (Oxford: Oxford University Press, 1984), 122-123.

[7] Barry Reay, *The Quakers and the English Revolution* (New York: St. Martin's Press, 1985), 9.

[8] Gordon Rupp, *Religion in England 1688-1791* (Oxford: Clarendon Press, 1986), 139.

[9] For this contact with Baptists, see Ingle, *First Among Friends*, 35-38, 42.

[10] *Journal of George Fox*, 11.

[11] *Ibid.*, 7.

[12] *Ibid.*, 33.

[13] Michael R. Watts, *The Dissenters* (Oxford: Clarendon Press, 1978), I, 203; T. L. Underwood, *Primitivism, Radicalism, and the Lamb's War: The Baptist-Quaker Conflict in Seventeenth-Century England* (New York/Oxford: Oxford University Press, 1997), 105-111.

[14] *Journal of George Fox*, 34-35. See the comments of Underwood on this passage: *Primitivism, Radicalism, and the Lamb's War*, 112.

[15] Cited Reay, *Quakers and the English Revolution*, 33.

[16] Hugh Barbour, *The Quakers in Puritan England* (New Haven/London: Yale University Press, 1964), 45; Arthur O. Roberts, 'George Fox and the Quakers' in John D. Woodbridge, ed., *Great Leaders of the Christian Church* (Chicago: Moody Press, 1988), 273.

[17] *The Inheritance of Jacob* (1656) in *Early Quaker Writings*, ed. Hugh Barbour and Arthur O. Roberts (Grand Rapids: William B. Eerdmans Publ. Co., 1973), 173.

[18] Reay, *Quakers and the English Revolution*, 27-29.

[19] Barbour, *Quakers in Puritan England*, 67-70.

[20] B. G. Reay, 'Early Quaker Activity and Reactions to it, 1652-1664' (Unpublished D. Phil. Thesis, University of Oxford, 1979), 218-220; *idem, Quakers and the English Revolution*, 26-27; Underwood, *Primitivism, Radicalism, and the Lamb's War*, 10.

[21] Underwood, *Primtivism, Radicalism, and the Lamb's War*, 105-107.

[22] *Ibid.*, 26-27, 32-33.

[23] Cited *ibid.*, 26.

[24] *Let Your Words Be Few*, 24-25.

[25] J. W. Frost, 'Penington, Isaac (the Younger)' in Richard L. Greaves and Robert Zaller, eds., *Biographical Dictionary of British Radicals in the Seventeenth Century* (Brighton, Sussex: The Harvester Press, 1984), III, 23.

[26] *Letters of Isaac Penington* (2nd. ed.; repr. London: Holdsworth and Ball, 1829), 202-203. For access to this text I am indebted to Heinz G. Dschankilic of Cambridge, Ontario.

[27] See also the remarks by Richard Dale Land, 'Doctrinal Controversies of English Particular Baptists (1644-1691) as Illustrated by the Career and Writings of Thomas Collier' (Unpublished D. Phil. Thesis, Regent's Park College, Oxford University, 1979), 205-211.

[28] *Journal of George Fox*, 39-40.

[29] Cited Reay, *Quakers and the English Revolution*, 34.

[30] For a different perspective on this issue, see James L. Ash, Jr., ' 'Oh No, It is not the Scriptures!' The Bible and the Spirit in George Fox', *Quaker History*, 63, No. 2 (Autumn 1974), 94-107.

[31] For others, see *ibid.*, 35-37.

[32] Watts, *Dissenters*, I, 209.

[33] Cited Richard G. Bailey, 'The Making and Unmaking of a God: New Light on George Fox and Early Quakerism' in Michael Mullett, ed., *New Light on George Fox (1624 to 1691)* (York: William Sessions Limited, The Ebor Press, 1991), 114.

[34] For a succinct account of this event, see Watts, *Dissenters*, I, 209-211. See also Charles L. Cherry, 'Enthusiasm and Madness: Anti-Quakerism in the Seventeenth Century', *Quaker History*, 74, No.2 (Fall 184), 7-9.

[35] Geoffrey F. Nuttall, 'The Quakers and the Puritans' in his *The Puritan Spirit: Essays and Addresses* (London: Epworth Press, 1967), 170, 174-175.

[36] Maurice A. Creasey, 'Early Quaker Christology with special reference to the Teaching and Significance of Isaac Penington 1616-1679' (Unpublished Ph.D. thesis, University of Leeds, 1956), 158. Creasey's thesis has been extremely helpful in following Owen's overall critique of Quaker teaching. See *ibid.*, 154-158.

[37] *The Work of the Holy Spirit in Prayer* [*The Works of John Owen*, ed. William H. Goold (1850-1853 ed.; repr. Edinburgh: Banner of Truth Trust, 1965-1968), *Works*, IV, 331].

[38] *A Discourse concerning the Holy Spirit* (*Works*, III, 66).

[39] *Ibid.* (*Works*, III, 36-37). See also *A Defense of Sacred Scripture Against Modern Fanaticism*, trans. Stephen P. Westcott in John Owen, *Biblical Theology* (Pittsburgh, Pennsylvania: Soli Deo Gloria

Publications, 1994), 777, where he suggests that the Quakers, or as some called them, 'quiverers,' were moved 'by the power of the evil spirit.'

[40] *Of Communion with God the Father, Son, and Holy Ghost* (*Works*, II, 258).

[41] *The Nature of Apostasy* (*Works*, VII, 219-220).

[42] *Discourse concerning the Holy Spirit* (*Works*, III, 66).

[43] *Of Communion with God the Father, Son, and Holy Ghost* (*Works*, II, 257-258). On the crucial importance of the Trinity for Owen's theology, see Carl R. Trueman, *The Claims of Truth: John Owen's Trinitarian Theology* (Carlisle, Cumbria: Paternoster Press, 1998).

[44] This is readily available in an English translation by Stephen P. Westcott: *A Defense of Sacred Scripture Against Modern Fanaticism* in John Owen, *Biblical Theology*, 775-854. For the date of this treatise, see Donald K. McKim, 'John Owen's Doctrine of Scripture in Historical Perspective', *The Evangelical Quarterly*, 45 (1973), 198 and n.16. For general studies of Owen's doctrine of Scripture, see Stanley N. Gundry, 'John Owen on Authority and Scripture' in John D. Hannah, ed., *Inerrancy and the Church* (Chicago: Moody Press, 1984), 189-221; Sinclair B. Ferguson, *John Owen on the Christian Life* (Edinburgh: Banner of Truth Trust, 1987), 185-201; John Wesley Campbell, 'John Owen's Rule and Guide: A Study in the Relationship between the Word and the Spirit in the Thought of Dr John Owen' (Unpublished M.Th. thesis, Regent College, Vancouver, 1991).

[45] *God's Statesman*, 76, n.4.

[46] *Defense of Sacred Scripture*, 805-816.

[47] For this claim, see Underwood, *Primtivism, Radicalism, and the Lamb's War*, 28.

[48] *Defense of Sacred Scripture*, 781-782, 791.

[49] *Ibid.*, 790-791.

[50] *Works*, IV, 121. For further discussion of other aspects of this first chapter of Owen's *Defense of Sacred Scripture*, see Trueman, *Claims of Truth*, 67-71.

[51] *Defense of Sacred Scripture*, 793-798.

[52] Trueman, *Claims of Truth*, 65-66. The same linkage is made in *The Causes, Ways, and Means of Understanding the Mind of God as Revealed in his Word*, chapters I-III (*Works*, IV, 121-160).

[53] For the debate, see especially, Geoffrey F. Nuttall, *The Holy Spirit in Puritan Faith and Experience* (2nd ed.; repr. Chicago/London: University of Chicago Press, 1992), 75-89 and Richard L. Greaves, 'The Ordination Controversy and the Spirit of Reform in Puritan England', *Journal of Ecclesiastical History*, 21 (1970), 225-241.

[54] *Defense of Sacred Scripture*, 802, 803.

[55] Greaves, 'Ordination Controversy', 227. For further discussion of Owen's thought on the issue of the interpretation of Scripture, see Ferguson, *John Owen on the Christian Life*, 196-199; J. I. Packer, 'John Owen on Communication from God' in his *A Quest for Godliness: The Puritan Vision of the Christian Life* (Wheaton, Illinois: Crossway Books, 1990), 93-95; Campbell, 'John Owen's Rule and Guide', 153-207; Trueman, *Claims of Truth*, 84-90.

[56] *Defense of Sacred Scripture*, 806-814.

[57] *Ibid.*, 814.

[58] *Ibid.*, 822.

[59] *Ibid.*, 823-824. See also *ibid.*, 833-835.

[60] *Ibid.*, 824-825. Gundry ('John Owen on Authority and Scripture', 194) notes only the soteriological purpose of the Bible.

[61] *Defense of Sacred Scripture*, 828, 829. For a brief summary of Owen's conception of the purposes of Scripture, see Ferguson, *John Owen on the Christian Life*, 199-201.

[62] *Defense of Sacred Scripture*, 829-832, *passim*.

[63] *Ibid.*, 841-843.

[64] *Ibid.*, 846-847.

[65] For the Quaker notion of the 'Spirit in every man,' see Nuttall, *Holy Spirit*, 159-162.

[66] See Creasey, 'Early Quaker Christology', 164-165 and the texts quoted there. Cf. Owen's remarks in *Defense of Sacred Scripture*, 853:'there are remains, although feeble ones, of creation light surviving in all men, but I strongly refute the suggestion that these remnants may be in any degree saving.'

[67] ΧΡΙΣΤΟΛΟΓΙΑ: *or, a Declaration of the Glorious Mystery of the Person of Christ – God and Man* (*Works*, I, 172-173).

[68] *Defense of Sacred Scripture*, 848, 849.

[69] *Ibid.*, 850-854.

[70] *Ibid.*, 852.

[71] *Ibid.*, 852.

[72] *Works*, I, 74-75. On the Trinitarian foundation of Owen's thought here, see Trueman, *Claims of Truth*, 70-71.

[73] ΣΥΝΕΣΙΣ ΠΝΕΥΜΑΤΙΚΗ· or, *The Causes, Ways, and Means of Understanding the Mind of God as Revealed in his Word, with Assurance therein* (*Works*, IV, 159-160).

Chapter Six

JOHN OWEN'S DOCTRINE OF THE CHURCH

Graham Harrison is minister of
Emmanuel Evangelical Church,
Newport. He has been Lecturer in
Christian Doctrine at the London
Theological Seminary since its
commencement in 1977.

An especial society or congregation of believers, joined together according unto his mind with their officers, guides, or rulers, whom he hath appointed, which do or may meet together for the celebration of all the ordinances of divine worship, the professing and authoritatively proposing the doctrine of the gospel ...

*Works,*XV.223

JOHN OWEN'S DOCTRINE OF THE CHURCH

When called upon to address at the 1988 National Evangelical Anglican Congress the late Archbishop Robert Runcie in effect chided the assembled delegates for having neglected to do their ecclesiological homework. He went on to call them to give diligent attention to the doctrine of the church, which, he suggested, had been notably ignored by the evangelical faction within the Ecclesia Anglicana. Whether he was right or wrong in his reading of the contemporary evangelical scene is perhaps debatable and in any sense is beside the point of this paper. What none of his seventeenth century archiepiscopal predecessors would have been justifed in doing would have been to have brought a similar charge against the evangelicals inside or outside the Established Church. Ecclesiological debates, so it could be argued, were stuff of which the seventeenth century was made. Certainly the doctrine of the church largely occupies the four concluding volumes of the Gould edition of John Owen's collected *Works.*

That this was not the fruit of a theological mind-set preoccupied – some might say obsessed – with matters ecclesiological to the neglect of other equally important areas of theological controversy is proved by the fact that most of these treatises are of a responsive nature. They are replies to what Owen would perceive to be calumnies and misrepresentations of a position that had once held sway in the nation but that now had fallen upon hard times. For from 1662 onwards Owen and his fellow Nonconformists laboured under restrictions that were often cruel and always unfair. That he was able to fight his corner so know-ledgeably – and for the most part so eirenically – tells us much both about his intellectual brilliance and his true spirituality.

Rather than trawl through the several tracts and treatises on the subject that came from Owen's voluminous pen I intend in this paper to restrict myself very largely to one work which gives the essence of his distinctive teaching. I say 'one work', whereas in appearance it is two, separated into successive volumes of his *Works* and by several years in dates of publication. The more well known of the two *The true Nature of a Gospel Church and its Government*[1] was published posthumously in 1689 six years in fact after his death. It is described as 'The second part', the first part being *An Inquiry into the Original, Nature, Institution, Power, Order, and Communion of Evangelical Churches*[2]. This in turn had been occasioned by the controversy set in motion when the Dean of St. Paul's, Dr Edward Stillingfleet, preached and printed his sermon *On the Mischief of Separation*. Owen had responded with *A Brief Vindication of the Nonconformists from the Charge of Schism*[3], to which the Dean replied extensively in the *Unreasonableness of Separation; or an impartial account of the history, nature and pleas of the present separation from the communion of the Church of England*.

In his *Brief Vindication* Owen had summarized Stillingfleet's position thus:

The charge is, 'That all the Nonconformists, of one sort or another, – that is, Presbyterians and Independents, – are guilty of sin, of a sinful separation from the church of England' and therefore, as they live in a known sin, so they are the cause thereby of great evils, confusion, disturbances among ourselves, and of danger unto the whole protestant religion:[4]

But this later and more extensive reply to Stillingfleet, together with its more well-known posthumous 'second part' represents Owen's definitive position.

But before we consider the sometimes detailed and involved argument that Owen advances in order to counter the charges of Stillingfleet and others it will be helpful to step back and view the wider perspective of Owen's life.

What makes him such an interesting, not to say fascinating, character in connection with his ecclesiological views can be stated very simply. Here was a man, arguably theologically the most able of his or most other generations, who was willing repeatedly to buck the trend of current opinion. That cost him a great deal in terms of worldly advancement and comfort. *Odium theologicum* was certainly not a commodity in short supply in mid and late seventeenth century England and Owen was on the receiving end of more than his fair share of it. Many Presbyterians regarded his avowal of Independency as little more than a running sore in the otherwise healthy body-Reformed. Anglicanism, whether in its earlier Laudian variety which caused him to leave Oxford or in its later seemingly more latitudinarian but in reality more vengeful and tyrannical form, recognised him as an adversary to be suppressed. But in it all he displayed a true catholicity of spirit allied to an earnest desire to conform to the Word of God. As a controversialist he was targeted by eminent and skilful opponents but rarely vanquished. Courteous in such controversy, he was a perceptive opponent whose logic would be penetrating and whose argumentation while occasionally caustic in its expression was seldom personal or vindictive – and that in an age when theological pugilists were used to bare-knuckle fighting.

Born into an episcopalian church but to a Puritan father (to whom afterwards he would attach the epithet *Nonconformist*) he was a convinced Presbyterian until 1644. But let him tell his own story:

I professed myself of the presbyterian judgement, in opposition to democratical confusion; and, indeed, so I do still, and so do all the congregational men in England that I am acquainted withal.

Of the congregational way I was not acquainted with any one person, minister or other; nor had I, to my knowledge, seen any more than one in my life. My acquaintance lay wholly with ministers and people of the presbyterian way. But sundry books being published on either side, I perused and compared them with the Scripture and one another, according as I received ability from God. After a general view of them, as was my manner in other controversies, I fixed on one to take under peculiar consideration and examination, which seemed most methodically and strongly to maintain that which was contrary, as I thought, to my present persuasion. This was Mr Cotton's book of the Keys.[5] In the pursuit and management of this work, quite beside and contrary to my expectation, at a time and season wherein I could expect nothing on that account but ruin in this world, without the knowledge or advice of, or conference with, any one person of that judgement, I was prevailed on to receive that and those principles which I had thought to have set myself in an opposition unto. And, indeed, this way of impartial examining all things by the word, comparing causes with causes and things with things, laying aside all prejudicate respects unto persons or present traditions, is a course that I would admonish all to beware of who would avoid the danger of being made Independents.[6]

It is clear that he understood Presbyterianism, both in its milder and more severe varieties. Indeed, some have argued that the form of Independency which he advocated at the end of his life was scarcely distinguishable from a moderate Presbyterianism. Gould, the nineteenth century editor of Owen's works vigorously denies this accusation: 'It is only, however, by a process of torture to which no man's language should be subjected that Owen can be claimed a Presbyterian.'[7] But more of this later. The issues over which he fought and for which he suffered are still with us. Are his arguments – or even his methods – still valid? To answer that question we must follow Owen's presentation of his case in this bipartite treatise.

When considering what he calls '*the original, nature, use, and end* (of churches), my first inquiry' he writes, 'must be whether they are from heaven or of men'[8]. This is foundational to all that Owen will argue subsequently. Basically he has already stated his fundamental thesis in the preface. What he is concerned to enquire into is '… the gospel church-state, as instituted, determined, and limited by our Lord Jesus Christ and his apostles' (p.194).

One thing he is at pains to point out is that Stillingfleet is wrong in representing his view of church government as being 'democratical' – 'which is a great mistake; I never thought, I never wrote any such thing' (p. 194). He continues 'I do believe that the authoritative rule or government of the church was, is, and ought to be, in the elders and rulers of it, being an act of the office-power committed unto them by Christ himself.' But significantly he adds immediately, 'Howbeit, my judgement is, that they ought not to rule their church with force, tyranny, and corporal penalties, or without their consent …' (p.194f.).

What Owen has to account for is how something like diocesan episcopacy ever came into the church if, as he vigorously will maintain, it was never instituted by Christ or the apostles. His answer is that it '... was introduced by insensible degrees, according unto the effectual working of the mystery of iniquity' (p.195) '... (which) began to work in the days of the apostles themselves, in the suggestions of Satan and the lusts of men, though in a manner latent and imperceptible unto the wisest Owen as 'the negligence of the people, and the ambition of the clergy' (p. 198).

He then expands on this in an interesting way. Stillingfleet had argued that it is altogether improbable that the people would have surrendered their interest in the government of the churches if they had ever had it, without 'great noise and trouble' – of which there is not the remotest trace in early church history (p. 200). Owen points to several factors that would have influenced the churches away from their original state. Among these were an excessive veneration for their bishops or pastors which led them to 'comply with their mistakes'. Also the numerical growth in the individual congregations coupled with the dangers to which their meeting together often exposed them resulted in the ordinary members forgoing their responsibilities and in effect looking to their leaders to perform them. Add to this a diminution in the holiness in the people and a love of pre-eminence on the part of the clergy and the scene was set for the emergence of 'popes, patriarchs, cardinals, metropolitan and diocesan bishops, who were utterly foreign into the state and order of the primitive churches, and that for some ages' (p.202). Its beginnings were small and it was done gradually but by the third and fourth century the original parity amongst elders had started to disappear. The situation was made worse by the emerging dominance of city churches and the subordination, often willingly, of the country churches to them.

Owen then leaps across the centuries to bring the situation up to date as far as the Church of England was concerned. He is at pains to point out that the Protestant Reformers, great as they were and amazing as was the work which under God they accomplished, were not infallible. They neither attained ecclesiastical perfection themselves, nor, for that matter, did they always agree among themselves regarding some of the issues 'now under contest'. Moreover, Reformed churches differed among themselves. All of which was not surprising given '*the horrid darkness* which they were newly delivered from' (p. 208). It is not, therefore, schism to dissent from a Church of England which insists upon imposing things that have no 'divine institution' or 'scriptural authority'. He summarises it thus:

> Those who charge schism on others for a dissent from themselves, or the refraining of total communion with them must... Give a farther confirmation than what we have yet seen unto the principles or presumptions they proceed upon in the management of the charge of schism; as that, – (l.) *Diocesan bishops,* with their *metropolitans,* are of divine institution; (2.) That the power of *rule* in and over all churches is committed unto them alone; (3.) That the church hath power to *ordain* religious rites and ceremonies nowhere prescribed in the Scripture, and impose the observation of them on all members of the church; (4.) That *this church* they are; (5.) That no man's *voluntary consent* is required to constitute him a member of any church, but that every one is surprised into that state whether he will or no; (6.) That there is *nothing* of force in the arguments pleaded for non-compliance with arbitrary unnecessary impositions; (7.) That the church standeth in no need of *reformation,* neither in doctrine, discipline, nor conversation; with sundry other things of an alike nature that they need unto their justification (p.214f).

Now it is fundamental to Owen's whole position that 'The original of this church-state is directly, immediately, and solely from
Jesus Christ, he alone is the author, contriver, and institutor of
it. ...he employed his apostles to act under him and from him in
the carrying on that work unto perfection. But what was done
by them is esteemed to be done all by himself' (p.234). He
continues:

> This, therefore, is absolutely denied by us, – namely,
> that any men, under what pretence or name soever, have
> any right or authority to constitute any new frame or
> order of the church, to make any laws of their own for
> its rule or government that should oblige the disciples
> of Christ in point of conscience unto their observation
> (p.238).

This New Testament church-state has been appointed by Christ
in perpetuity. The temporary and extraordinary offices of apostles and evangelists have ceased and the continuing existence
of the church is in no way dependent on such a continuance. Its
officers depend on it, not it on them, as Roman theory and the
Anglicanism against which Owen was contending, maintained.
'Yea,' he rather acidly comments, 'some of the men of this
persuasion, [think] that Christians cannot be saved unless they
comply with their diocesan bishops, do yet grant that heathens
might be saved without the knowledge of Christ!' (p.253).
Perhaps we should add that the species is not yet quite extinct!

     In one of the most important sections of the treatise Owen
gives attention to what he calls 'the especial nature of the
gospel church-state appointed by Christ'. He explicitly sides steps
the argument for a national church-state based on classical and
provincial assemblies (i.e. Presbyterianism) in order to concentrate on 'the visible church-state which Christ hath instituted
under the New Testament'. This, he continues, consists in

an especial society or congregation of professed believers, joined together according unto his mind, with their officers, guides, or rulers, whom he hath appointed, which do or may meet together for the celebration of all the ordinances of divine worship, the professing and authoritatively proposing the doctrine of the gospel, with the exercise of the discipline prescribed by himself unto their own mutual edification, with the glory of Christ, in the preservation and propagation of his kingdom in the world (p.262).

What he is arguing for is that the church consists of visible believers, voluntarily joining together in a congregation in a locality to practise the ordinances and institutions of Christ, preaching the word, administering the sacraments and exercising gospel discipline, all in subjection to Christ. Such a congregation will be neither too small to fulfil all these functions nor too large to prevent them from gathering together. It will consist in its complete state of pastors, or a pastor and ruling elders ruling over a community of the faithful. To such a church belong all the privileges, promises and power granted by Christ (p.262).

The ends for which Christ has appointed this church-state are three-fold: the professed subjection of the souls and consciences of believers to Christ's authority in observing his commands, the joint celebration of gospel ordinances and worship, and the exercise and preservation of Christ's discipline by maintaining the purity of the gospel, preserving love among Christians, and representing Christ's love in and through the church.

And, he adds, 'it is in congregational churches alone that these things can be done and observed; for unto all of them there are required assemblies of the whole church, which, wherever they are, that church is congregational. No such churches … – papal, patriarchal, metropolitical, diocesan, or in any way national – are capable of the discharge of these duties or attaining of these ends' (p.268). As he puts it a little later, ' although the essence of the church doth not consist in actual assemblies, yet, are they absolutely necessary unto its constitution in exercise' (p.269).

The Hebrew and Greek terms for gathering, assembly, church, together with an extended discussion of Mt. 18:17 all provide him with material that he uses to substantiate his position. His summary of our Lord's words regarding church discipline in Mt. 18 consolidate his case.

> It is plain in the place, – (1.) That there was a church-state for Christians then designed by Christ, which afterward he would institute and settle; (2.) That all true disciples were to join and unite themselves in some such church as might be helpful unto their love, order, peace, and edification; (3.) That among the members of these churches offences would or might arise, which in themselves tend unto pernicious events; (4.) That if these offences could not be cured and taken away, so as that love without dissimulation might be continued among all the members of the churches, an account of them at last was to be given unto that church or society whereunto the parties concerned do belong as members of it; (5.) That this church should hear, determine, and give judgement, with advice, in the cases so brought unto it, for the taking away and removal of all offences; (6.) That this determination of the church is to be rested in, on the penalty of a deprivation of all the privileges of the church; (7.) That these things are the institution and appointment of Christ himself whose authority in them all is to be submitted unto, and which alone can cast one that is a professed Christian into the condition of a heathen or a publican (p.274).

Owen then moves on to assert that for two centuries after Christ the churches were congregational and knew no other form of church government. There was variety amongst them – variety with regard to gifts, reputation, situation – but this variety in no way impinged upon the equality that prevailed. Clement of Rome, Polycarp, Ignatius, Justin Martyr are amongst those to whom he refers in support of his thesis. But, he continues, 'From this state the churches did by degrees insensibly degenerate, so as another form and order of them did appear towards the end of the third century' (p.299).

The remainder of this treatise is largely taken up with a practical application of these principles to Owen's contemporary scene. As might be expected it is, in effect, an *apologia pro vita sua*. Congregational churches alone meet the ends for which Christ has instituted his church (p. 302ff). Such churches are distinct from the state and yet constitute no threat to it (p.309). The very concept of a 'national church' is something that he simply cannot countenance (p.315), for to do so would be to deprive the local congregation of the powers with which Christ himself has invested them (p.313).

Believers, therefore, have an obligation to join themselves to such local congregations both for God's glory as well as their own edification (p. 319f.). As he puts it, 'it is the indispensable duty of every disciple of Christ, in order unto his edification and salvation, voluntarily, and of his own choice, to join himself in and unto some particular congregation, for the celebration of divine worship, and the due observation of all the institutions and commands of Christ ...' (p.325). But that immediately raises the question as to what sort of churches ought Christ's disciples to join themselves in entire communion.

He has a very interesting section (chapter X, pp. 334-344) in which he freely recognises that churches differ. Some differences and division came as the result of what he calls 'the remaining weaknesses, infirmities, and ignorance of the best of men' but some result from disagreements 'about things *fundamental* in faith, worship, and obedience' (p.335). Thus where 'any *fundamental* article of faith is rejected or corrupted' the believer is not bound to join with such a church. Likewise churches that teach or allow 'a mixture of doctrines or opinions that are prejudicial unto gospel holiness and obedience' ought not to be joined. Rome is ruled out because it has corrupted or overthrown the fundamentals of religious worship.

Putting it all positively, the disciple of Christ is to join a church which functions in reality as the pillar and ground of the truth (p.339). Wranglings and contentions about fundamental truths of the gospel simply subvert the souls of men. There is a 'variety in apprehensions in some doctrines of lesser moment' about which mutual forbearance should be exercised – although intriguingly Owen does not spell out what these might be! Divine worship as instituted or approved by Christ is another positive condition Owen is looking for – no additions or subtractions. Finally, no man can consider himself to be obliged to join himself to a church where the ministry is not conducive to the edification of believing souls. 'let men cry out 'schism' and 'faction' whilst they please' he writes, 'Jesus Christ will acquit his disciples in the exercise of their liberty, and accept them in the discharge of their duty' (p.342). Interestingly enough, however, earlier in this same chapter he speaks about a 'peaceable departure': 'That this be done peaceably, without strife or contention, without judging of others, as unto their interest in Christ and eternal salvation, the law of moral obedience doth require; that it be done with love, and compassion, and prayer towards and for them who are left, is the peculiar direction of that moral duty by the gospel' (p.338). Would that such an injunction had been heeded in more recent years!

All this is leading up to the real issue that has occasioned the treatise. Is dissent from the Church of England schism? Owen's answer will be obvious. To dissent from it 'is no more schism than it is adultery' (p.346). Indeed, dissent is something virtually forced upon the faithful believer because the absolute insistence on his submitting to all the canon law and the rubric of the Book of Common Prayer, backed up as it was by the law of the land, deprived the Christian man of his liberty. He instances the case of the sign of the cross in baptism being insisted upon, otherwise a man is regarded as a schismatic. His comment is unadorned and all the more effective because of it: ' I shall only say that I am not of their mind, nor ever shall be so' (p.347).

The chapter concludes with six assertions which make up Owen's reasons for dissent:

1. In its parochial assemblies the Church of England stands in need of reformation. When a church wilfully refuses to reform itself then Christ threatens to withdraw his presence. 'It is safer leaving of any church whatever than of Jesus Christ' (p.350). He goes so far as to say that the Church of England 'doth not, and it is to be feared, *will not, nor can reform itself* (p.352).

2. 'The constitution of these parochial assemblies (i.e. parish churches) is not from heaven, but of men' (p.354).

3. 'There is not in them ... *a fixed standard of truth*, or rule of faith to be professed ...' (p.375). Thus the XXXIX Articles needed supplementing if only to take account of heresies like Socinianism and Arminianism which simply were not around when the Articles were first formulated. But instead of the Articles regulating belief 'such novel opinions about the person, grace, satisfaction and righteousness of Christ, about the work of the Holy Spirit of God in regeneration, or the renovation of our nature into the image of God ...' abound in some churches (p. 358).

4. 'Evangelical discipline is neither observed nor attainable in these parochial assemblies' (p. 358). Instead 'a secular power

is erected, coercive by pecuniary and corporal penalties, administered by persons in no way relating unto the churches over which they exercise their power, by rules of human laws and constitutions, in litigious and oppressive courts, in the room of that institution of Christ, whose power and exercise is spiritual, by spiritual means, according to spiritual rules ...' (p.360).

5. The people no longer enjoy their God-given right of choice of all their church officers, but rather patrons and others can impose a minister on them.

6. Furthermore, public assent and consent to the Book of Common Prayer, with its rubric is required, and a renunciation of all other ways of public worship demanded. To summarize:

> On these suppositions, I say, the imposition of the things so often contended about on the consciences and profession of Christians, – as, namely, the constant, sole use of the liturgy in all church administrations, in the matter and manner prescribed; the use and practice of all canonical ceremonies; the religious observation of stated holidays, with other things of the like nature, – is sufficient to warrant any sober, peaceable disciple of Christ, who takes care of his own edification and salva-tion, to refrain the communion required in this rule of conformity, unless he be fully satisfied in his own mind that all that it requires is according to the mind of Christ, and all that it forbids is disapproved by him (p.364).

But lest the reader be tempted at this point to think that Owen sits loosely by the sin of schism he makes it clear that 'Schism is a sin against christian love' (p.365).

If the first part of this treatise might be reminiscent at times of conflicts long since confined to history the same certainly cannot be said of the second part. *The True Nature of a Gospel Church* debates issues that are still on the theological agenda whenever matters of ecclesiology are discussed. What some might regard as the mixed blessing that the rediscovery of the concept of eldership in reformed Baptist circles has been could be adduced as witness to that fact. Certainly this work of Owen's has become one of the foundation documents of classic Independency even if 'democratical' elements that do not lie too easily with Owen's basic position have come to occupy the same bed!

The basic position that Owen has sought to establish in the first part is briefly stated by him in his Preface: 'There is no other sort of visible church of Christ organized ... but a particular church or congregation (either in the Old or New Testament) where all the members thereof do ordinarily meet together in one place to hold communion one with another in some one or more great ordinances of Christ' (p. 3). He writes, 'It is absurd to say that a man is a visible husband to an invisible wife; the relate and correlate must be "eiusdem naturae".' Therefore pastors and other church do officers do not range freely over the catholic church at large. Rather, 'the church must be visible to which he is an officer (p.5). A credible profession of faith and holiness is the foundation of a visible church; men and women, not doctrine, constitute its matter and they are united together not by internal and invisible bonds of the Spirit, but by visible bonds of union. Thus 'a gospel church is a company of faithful, professing people, walking together by mutual consent or confederation to the Lord Jesus Christ and one to another, in subjection to and practice of all his gospel precepts and commands, whereby they are separate from all persons and things manifestly contrary or disagreeing thereunto' (p.6). That is the position that Owen sets out to confirm and elaborate.

As might be expected Owen immediately takes up the question of church membership. What are the qualifications required of aspiring church members? Regeneration is expressly required in the gospel, he maintains, citing Jn. 3:3, Titus 3:3-5 in support. This does not consist in 'any outward rite, easy to be observed by the worst and vilest of men' (p.12), even though baptism is its symbol, sign, expression and representation. God alone is the infallible judge of its reality but the church must judge its evidences and fruits in their external demonstration.

Consequently there are some who on no account are to be admitted into the fellowship of the church, and Owen refers to 1 Cor. 6:9-11, Phil. 3:18f, 2 Thess. 3:6, 2 Tim. 3:5 to prove this: 'a man known to live in sin cannot regularly be received into any church'. To admit such 'is not to erect temples to Christ but chapels unto the devil' (p.13).

Similarly, church members are to be admonished of any scandalous sin and cast out if they will not repent. He goes on to emphasise the importance of an open profession of the subjection of their souls and consciences to the authority of Christ in the gospel, and their readiness to yield obedience to all his commands. For such a profession to be credible a certain amount of 'competent knowledge of the doctrine and mystery of the gospel, especially concerning the person and offices of Christ' is needed. 'The promiscuous driving of all sorts of persons who have been baptised in their infancy unto a participation of all church privileges is a profanation of the holy institutions of Christ' (p.15). Subjection to Christ's authority, self denial and cross bearing are essential, as is conviction and confession of sin. Significantly he adds at this point 'with the way of deliverance by Jesus Christ' (p.17), quoting 1 Peter 3:21 in support. The constant performance of all known duties of religion and a careful abstinence from all known sins, giving scandal or offence either to the world or to the church complete the list.

The judgement exercised will be a judgement of charity. Those who pass these stringent tests but yet are 'not real living members of the mystical body of Christ ... are ... meet members of that body of Christ unto which he is a head of rule and government ...' (p. 17). The trouble is that following the Roman emperors' embracing the Christian religion multitudes were admitted into churches on a bare, outward profession of faith. Sadly until the much vilified Calvin tightened things up in Geneva Protestantism continued the same policy. But even in this, he maintains, we see God's providential care, for had the first Reformers operated on this principle they might 'have greatly obstructed, if not utterly defeated, their endeavour for the reformation of doctrine and worship.' (p.20).

But that leads him on to consider the implications of this for joining churches whose members are 'visibly unholy and which make no attempt to apply in the judgement of charity those principles which he has been enumerating. Owen's answer is unequivocal: 'It is the duty of every member who takes care of his present edification and the future salvation of his soul peaceably to withdraw from the communion of such churches, and to join in such others where all the ends of church-societies may in some manner be obtained' (p.22).

What Owen has been leading up to is a discussion of the place of discipline amongst a covenanted community that each has entered by his or her voluntary consent. In the discussion that follows he has two targets in mind. First of all, that which deriving from Rome was still present in the Church of England – the tyrannical and oppressive, not to say coercive, exercise of discipline over men's persons and possessions. But at the same time he surely has his eye on the lesser target represented by some of the more severe advocates of Presbyterianism.

In contrast to both he wants to insist that 'there is no rule of the church but what is *ministerial,* consisting in an *authoritative declaration* and application of the commands and will of Christ unto the souls of men' (p.33). Edification is always the aim in the exercise of ministerial power, never 'lordly domination'.

Owen, of course, was a cessationist and clearly held to the position that the extraordinary church-power committed by Christ to his apostles has not been granted to the continuing church. Instead this whole church-power is now committed to the whole church by Christ and it is communicated by his word and Spirit. This is something to which he will return and take up in more detail later, but first he turns his attention to the officers of the church.

There are two sorts – bishops and deacons. Bishops, or elders, are further subdivided into those who both teach and rule, and those who only rule. The former again are divided by Owen into two – pastors and teachers. Clearly there is no diocesan episcopal hierarchy in mind here. He will have none of the view that there is a superiority of bishops or presbyters in order or degree. 'in the whole New Testament bishops and presbyters, or elders, are every way the same persons, in the same office, have the same function, without distinction in order or degree ...' (p.44).

He then proceeds to employ what have long since become the standard arguments for both the parity and plurality of elders, after which he makes the following observation: 'Those whose names are the same, equally common and applicable unto them all, whose function is the same, whose qualification and characters are the same, concerning whom there is in no one place of Scripture the least mention of inequality, disparity, or preference in office among them, they are essentially and every way the same' (p.45f).

But this does not preclude the possibility that given a plurality of elders one may preside and guide in their deliberation. However, such a person occupies no new and superior ecclesiastical order, nor does he possess a new degree of power or authority in the church. 'The Scripture knows no more of an archbishop, such as all diocesan bishops are, nor an archdeacon, than of an archapostle, or an archevangelist, or an archprophet' (p.46).

He has a very telling section in which he describes the pastoral office. The very term is descriptive of the work the pastor should do and the person he should be – a shepherd who feeds the flock with love, care, tenderness and watchfulness. These

characteristics together with a zeal for the glory of God will be
pointers as to the validity of his call.

A man is not to intrude himself into this office (Heb. 5:4),
but rather is to be called by the church. This will involve first of
all Election and then Ordination. Having duly considered his
spirituality and his gifts, it is the church that has the power of
election. The elders, who may have taken advice of other elders
and churches, will in turn advise the 'fraternity' (presumably
the men) who, together with the elders, will exercise their common suffrage. At this point he has an interesting discussion of
the case of Matthias in Acts 1. 'As he had to be a church officer
he had the choice and consent of the church; but as he was to
be an apostle or an extraordinary officer, there was an immediate
divine disposition of him into his office' (p. 56) – which is an
interesting piece of exegesis. Acts 14:25 he interprets as
confirming common suffrage in the appointments of elders.

What he is talking about is, in the ecclesiological parlance
common in the seventeenth century, 'the power of the keys'
(p. 63). It had been John Cotton's *The Keyes of the Kingdom
of Heaven* (1644) that had effectively turned this one time Presbyterian into the champion of Independency. The keys, he
maintains, are given to the whole church, although their power
is exercised ministerially by the elders.

But the person thus elected to office has to be installed into
it, which is where the subject of ordination comes to the fore.
Accompanied by fasting and prayer 'The conduct of this work
belongs to the elders or officers of the church wherein any one
is to be so ordained' (p. 73). He is happy with the laying on of
hands, provided that 'there be no apprehension of its being the
sole authoritative conveyance of a successive flux of office-
power, which is destructive of the whole nature of the institution' (p.73).

In common with the invariable opinion of his Puritan brethren, Owen had a very high view of the pastoral calling. To

describe preaching as something of a hobby or as an occasional diversionary activity engaged in by men who could preach but who preferred to spend their lives doing more important things was inconceivable to Owen. 'Nor is it required only that he preach now and then at his leisure, but that he lay aside all other employments, though lawful, all other duties in the church, as unto such constant attendance on them would divert him from this work, that he gave himself unto it, – that he be in these things labouring to the utmost of his ability' (p. 75).

A preacher must be a man of fervent prayer for 'without this, no man can or doth preach to them as he ought' (p.77). To him is committed the administration of the seals of the covenant. This causes Owen to raise the question as to whether a pastorless church can appoint one of its members to administer the ordinances. His answer is decidedly in the negative. Such a church is incomplete without teaching officers. 'The practice therefore proposed is irregular, and contrary to the mind of Christ' (p.80).

The pastors have to preserve and defend the truth of the gospel against all opposition and this will involve them not only in knowing and loving the doctrine but also in being fully aware of erroneous views. They will labour for the conversion of souls to God in which the chief means will be the preaching of the word. Normally this will be done in the context of his own congregation although Owen does allow for the possibility of occasional preaching elsewhere and exceptionally: 'it is the duty of pastors of particular churches to leave their constant attendance on their pastoral charge in those churches, at least for a season, to apply themselves to the more public preaching of the word unto the conversion of the souls of men' (p. 85). He has a reference to the good shepherd leaving the ninety and nine sheep to seek after the one that wanders. 'we may certainly leave a few for a season, to seek after a great multitude of wanderers, when we are called thereunto by divine providence.'

Then intriguingly he adds, 'and I could heartily wish that we might have a trial of it at this time' (p. 85).

There are a number of other points that are worth pulling together from this section. firstly, one church is enough for one pastor (p.90). Secondly, if you are faced with a 'defective or neglective' pastor and there is no way to remove him, then it is perfectly in order to vote with your feet and, with the edification of your soul in view, join with a church where there is no such problem. Thirdly, he denies that a church has the power to *ordain* men ministers '*for the conversion of infidels*' (p. 93). Since the cessation of extraordinary officers and offices that has to be left to the providence of God; 'but it is not in the power of any church, or any set of ordinary officers, to ordain a person unto the office of the ministry for the conversion of the heathen antecedently unto any designation by divine providence thereunto' (p. 93).

Owen rather concessively allows that there may be 'just causes' of the removal of a pastor from one congregation to another. However, generally speaking a pastor should not voluntarily resign – certainly he should not do so on account of weakness brought on by age or sickness, nor on account of weariness and despondency under opposition. However, an incurable decay of intellectual abilities, incurable divisions in the church, a failure on the part of the congregation to give the necessary material support and also 'if he be pressed in point of conscience' (p.96), these would be grounds for resignation.

The office of teacher as distinct from that of pastor is one that Owen, in common with Calvin, maintains to be valid and necessary. He tries to argue, I think unsuccessfully, from Ephesians 4:11 for a distinction between pastor and teacher. And in an unusual instance that possibly can be attributed to even Homer nodding, he argues that the presence of such in the church at Alexandria at the end of the second century ' had never been so exactly practised in the church if it had not

derived from divine institution' (p. 100) – which seems poten-
tially to open the door to innumerable undesirable practices.
But he does admit that controversy surrounds the whole issue.

Two chapters, VII and VIII, are devoted to the question of
elders. first of all Owen elaborates his convictions regarding
ruling elders. All elders rule, but in addition to ruling some also
labour in the word and doctrine. 1 Tim. 5:17 is the text to which
Owen will direct our attention. It goes without saying that he
will reject the concept of chancellors and the like, but ruling
elders – that is, men ordained to the office of elder, but who
function only in a ruling capacity – he sees as a Scriptural
provision for the due administration of 'the keys of the kingdom'. It is something different from the pastoral work of preaching and administering the sacraments and it requires different
gifts. Although some men may possess both gifts, most do not.
Owen hastens to add that pastors and teachers are not divested
of the right of rule in the church (p.111), but that the work of
prayer and preaching is 'ordinarily sufficient to *take up the whole
man* ...' (p. 110).

Owen reduces his exegesis of 1 Tim. 5:17 to a syllogism:

'Preaching elders, although they rule well, are not worthy
of double honour, unless they labour in the word and
doctrine;
    But there are elders who rule well that are worthy of
double honour, though they do not labour in the word and
doctrine:
    Therefore there are elders that rule well who are not
teaching or preaching elders, – that is, who are ruling
elders only' (p. 118f).

In fact he affirms (p. 112) that the Jerusalem elders mentioned
in Acts 11:30 must have been ruling elders as the teaching was
still in the hands of the apostles.

But what Owen is maintaining repeatedly is that it is at least
highly desirable that any particular church has many elders, at

least more than one (p. 112). How many will depend on the size of the congregation. 'But that church, be it small or great, is not complete in its state, is defective, which hath not more elders than one, which hath not so many as are sufficient for their work' (p. 112). On the basis of Deut. 1:15 he suggests one elder for every ten persons or families (p.114).

It is commonly assumed that Independency is church government on a democratic basis. Certainly as far as many modern Congregational and Baptist churches are concerned they suffer from what someone has called 'the tyranny of the 51 per cent'. But nothing could be further from Owen's conception of church government. It had been one of his arguments in favour of a plurality of elders that 'It is difficult, if not impossible, on a supposition of one elder only in a church, to preserve the rule of the church from being *prelatical* or *popular*' (p. 112). *Democratical* is the synonym he uses earlier for *popular*. If the one is Scylla then the other is Charybdis and it really does not make much difference in terms of which alternative you make shipwreck of the church.

But Owen endeavours to show that 'the necessary consent of the people' for which he will contend does not lead to a *democratical* form of church government. 'the work of the fraternity is not determining and authoritative, but only declarative of consent and obedience' (p. 131). The power of the keys lies with the elders, otherwise 'it overthrows all that beautiful order which Jesus Christ hath ordained.' What is at stake here is the kingly office of Christ. His point is that ruling on the part of the elders is something that must be done spiritually and, to use the word that occurs so frequently in this connection in Owen, *ministerial*. If the law is spiritual so must its administration be. Great responsibility therefore rests on the elders always to function in accordance with these principles. They will need great skill and practical wisdom as well as pastoral sensitivity in applying the law of Christ to the varying cases, or rather persons, with whom they have to deal.

The chapter dealing with deacons is much briefer. Their task is to care for the poor and the sick. Theirs is a permanent office in the church and he is careful to point out that it has nothing to do with *archdeacons*!

> And whereas, when all things were swelling with pride and ambition in the church ... there arose from the name of this office the meteor of an archdeacon, with strange powers and authority, never heard of in the church for many ages, this belongs unto the mystery of iniquity, whereunto neither the Scripture nor the practice of the primitive churches doth give the least countenance (p.147).

Excommunication is the heading of the penultimate chapter of Owen's treatise. It is one of the longest and undoubtedly one of the most helpful. By definition, excommunication has to do with the members of the church and 'the exclusion from its society of such as obstinately refuse to live and walk according unto the laws and rules of it' (p. 151). From beginning to end it is something spiritual – its causes, its progress, its exercise, its revocation. Matthew 18:15-20 figures largely in Owen's account, together with 1 Cor. 5:1-7 and Acts 8: 13, 20-23. His comments on the Matthaean passage are worth noting:

> But that by 'trespasses' in this place, sins against God, giving scandal or offence, are intended, hath been proved before; as also, that by 'church' a particular Christian congregation is intended. This church hath the cognizance of the scandalous offences of its members committed unto it, when brought before it in the due order described. Hereon it makes a determination, designing in the first place the recovery of the person offending from his sin, by his hearing of its counsel and advice; but, in case of obstinacy, it is to remove him from its

communion, leaving him in the outward condition of a 'heathen man and a publican:' so is he to be esteemed by them that were offended with his sin; and that because of the authority of the church binding him in heaven and earth unto the punishment due unto his sin, unless he doth repent. The rejection of an offending brother out of the society of the church, leaving him, as unto all the privileges of the church, in the state of a heathen, declaring him liable unto the displeasure of Christ and everlasting punishment, without repentance, is the excommunication we plead for; and the power of it, with its exercise, is here plainly granted by Christ and ordained in the church (p.160).

Owen is adamant that there is only one sort of excommunication, not two, the 'lesser' and the 'greater' – as some supposed to have been the case among the Jews. '*A segregation from all participation in church order*, worship and privileges, is the only excommunication spoken of in the Scripture (p.165). Suspension from the Lord's Table prior to full examination is 'only an act of prudence in church-rule, to avoid offence and scandal'.

It is essential that the whole church be involved in the act of excommunication, because the practical execution of the sentence rests with the body of the church: 'Wherefore, excommunication without the consent of the church is a nullity' (p.167). Those who are the subjects of excommunication will be church members who obstinately continue in scandalous sin after private and public admonition. The offence must be clearly recognized and acknowledged by all and confessed or clearly proved. The censure will not be undertaken in haste and certainly not with eagerness, but only after patient but futile admonition. It will be proceeded with lamentation, a due sense of the future judgement of Christ and with the aim of restoration. 'The *nature* and *end* of this judgement or sentence being *corrective*, not *vindictive* ...' (p. 171).

Genuine repentance will preclude excommunication but might still be followed by possible exclusion from the Lord's Table for a season as an act of 'rectorial prudence' (p. 177).

Owen's reluctance to embark on a policy of hasty excommunication is shown by the way in which he considers how much time is to be given after solemn admonition, before actual excommunication:

No present *appearance of obstinacy* or impenitence under admonition (which is usually pleaded) should cause an immediate procedure unto excommunication; for,–(1.) It is contrary unto the *distinct institution* of the one and the other (i.e. solemn admonition and actual excommunication), wherein the former is to be allowed its proper season for its use and efficacy. (2.) It doth not represent *the patience and forbearance of Christ towards his church* and all the members of it. (3.) It is not suited unto the rule of that love which 'hopeth all things, beareth all things,' etc. (4.) All grounds of hope for the recovery of sinners by repentance are to he attended unto, so as to defer the ultimate sentence (p.179).

The measure of Owen's pastoral and compassionate heart is seen in the way in which he answers a miscellany of practical questions that he raises towards the end of the chapter. For instance, Can excommunicated persons be admitted to the hearing of the word in the assemblies of the church? Yes! 'When persons are under this sentence, the church is in a state of expecting their recovery and return, and therefore are not to prohibit them any means thereof, such as is preaching of the word' (p.180).

What about 1 Corinthians. 5:11, 'with such an one no not to eat' and 1 Thessalonians. 3:14, 'Note that man, and have no company with him, that he may be ashamed'? Answer: 'Herein all ordinary converse of *choice*, not made necessary by previous occasions, is forbidden. No *suspension* of duties antecedently necessary by virtue of natural or moral relation is allowed or countenanced by this rule; such as those of husband and wife, parents and children, magistrates and subjects, masters and servants, neighbours, relations in propinquity or blood. No duties arising from or belonging unto any of these relations are released, or the obligation unto them weakened, by excommunication. Husbands may not hereon forsake their wives if they are excommunicated, nor wives their husbands ...' (p. 180).

Then Owen tackles the question as to how ought excommunicated persons to be received into the church upon their repentance? Answer: 'as unto the *internal manner*, with all readiness and cheerfulness, with, – Meekness, ... compassion with love in all the demonstrations of it ... with joy, to represent the heart of Christ towards repentant sinners' (p. 181). After stating the outward manner or the due process by which they are to be received he goes on to comment:

> But there may be an evil observed among some ... that they seek not after the recovery of those that are excommunicated, by prayer, admonition, exhortation, in a spirit of meekness and tenderness, but are well satisfied that they have quitted themselves of their society. It is better never to excommunicate any, than so to carry it towards them that are excommunicated. But there is a sort of men unto whom if a man once be an offender, he shall be so for ever (p.181).

Finally he makes it clear that in dubious or disputable cases or in the absence of due proof by positive witnesses no excommunication is allowed.

The concluding chapter deals with the communion of churches, or as we would put it today, inter-church relationships. No one reading it could possibly go away with the impression that Independency is a synonym for isolationism in

Owen's theological dictionary. On the contrary, some have even queried whether he can really be a true Independent and is not in fact a Presbyterian wolf masquerading in Independent sheep's clothing! But the charge will not stick.

He does not actually phrase it like this, but his argument initially proceeds in parallel with what he had to say regarding church officers. Just as there is a parity in that case, so there is here among the churches: 'there is an equality of power and order, though not of gifts and usefulness …' (p. 185). No ecclesiastical hierarchy here! Geography and the providence of God will prescribe the lines of communication, but from such communication no true church of Christ is or can be excluded (p.185). He spends a few pages deliberately excluding Rome from such a category and making the point explicitly that the Pope is the antichrist (p. 187).

It is a church's relation to Christ that is fundamental. Faith in Christ, love to Him, holiness, obedience to His commands – these are the requisites for this union between the churches. 'There may be failures in them or some of them, as unto sundry of these things; there may be differences among them, about them, arising from the infirmities, ignorance, and prejudices of them of whom they do consist, the best knowing here but in part; but whilst the substance of them is preserved, the union of all churches, and so of the catholic church, is preserved. This is the blessed oneness which the Lord Christ prayed for so earnestly for his disciples…' (109 f)

It is when Owen comes to deal with the vexed question of synods that he will find himself under attack from opposite sides. He bases his argument for their validity not on an express command in Scripture – for there is none – but on 'the nature of the thing itself' and on the apostolic example provided in Acts 15 – the so-called council of Jerusalem. Earlier he has stated that 'Churches have communion unto their mutual edification by advice in synods or councils' (p. 195).

He argues that this was simply the first church of the Jews (Jerusalem) and the first church of the Gentiles (Antioch) meeting through delegates 'to avoid or cure offences against mutual love among them' and 'to advance the light of the gospel by a joint conference and agreement in the faith' (p.199). He ridicules the idea that there ever has been or can be an ecumenical council in which all the particular churches of the world are represented. The trouble was that the pattern of the Roman Empire was adopted by the churches: 'So was the visible professing church moulded and fashioned into an image of the old Roman pagan empire, as it was foretold it should be, Revelation. 13: 13-15' (p. 201).

He is in favour of frequent synods: 'it were not amiss if those churches which do walk in express communion would *frequently meet in synods*, to enquire after the state of them all, and to give advice for the correction of what is amiss, the due preservation of the purity of worship, the exercise of discipline, but especially of the power, demonstration, and fruit of evangelical obedience' (p. 199).

The possibility of a national synod and lesser regional assemblies of likeminded churches is not ruled out by him, provided the rights of individual churches are not overridden by the synod assuming judicial powers over them. He ends with a brief treatment of the council of Jerusalem.

(1.) (Its) *occasion* … was a difference in the church of Antioch, which they could not compose among themselves, because those who caused the difference pretended authority from the apostles …

(2.) The *means of its convention* was the desire and voluntary reference of the matter in debate made by the church at Antioch, where the difference was, unto that at Jerusalem, where, as it was pretended, the cause of the difference arose, unto the hazard of their mutual communion, to be consulted of with their own messengers.

(3.) The *persons constituting the* synod were the apostles, elders, and brethren of the church at Jerusalem, and the messengers of that of Antioch, with whom Paul and Barnabas were joined in the same delegation.

(4.) The *matter* in difference was debated, as unto the mind of God concerning it in the *Scripture,* and out of the Scripture. On James' proposal the determination was made.

(5.) There was nothing *imposed anew* on the practice of the churches; only direction is given in one particular instance as unto duty, necessary on many accounts unto the Gentile converts, namely, to abstain from fornication and from the use of their liberty in such instances of its practice as whereon scandal would ensue; which was the duty of all Christians even before this determination, and is so still in many other instances besides those mentioned in the decree, only it was now declared unto them.

(6.) The *grounds* whereon the synod proposed the reception of and compliance with its decrees were four – [l.] 'It pleased the Holy Ghost' … and it is evident that it was … a discovery of the mind of the Holy Ghost in the Scripture, that is intended. However, it is concluded that nothing be proposed or confirmed in synods but what is well known to be the mind of the Holy Ghost in the Scripture, either by immediate inspiration or by Scripture revelation. [2.] The authority of the assembly, as convened in the name of Christ and by virtue of his presence, whereof we have spoken before: 'It pleased the Holy Ghost and us.' [3.] … the things … determined were 'necessary;' that is, antecedently so … [4.] From the duty with respect unto the peace and mutual communion of the Jewish and Gentile churches: 'Doing thus,' say they, 'ye shall do well;' which is all the sanction of their decree, manifesting that it was doctrinal, not authoritative in way of jurisdiction.

(7.) The doctrinal abridgment of the liberty of the Gentile Christians in case of scandal they call the 'imposing of no other burden' in opposition unto what they rejected, namely, the imposing a yoke of ceremonies upon them, verse 10: so that the meaning of these words is, that they would lay no burden on them at all, but only advise them unto things necessary for the avoidance of scandal; for it is impious to imagine that the apostles would impose any yoke or lay any burden on the disciples but only the yoke and burden of Christ, as being contrary to their commission, Matt. xxviii. 19, 20 (p.207f.).

From this Owen concludes: 'Hence it will follow that a synod convened in the name of Christ, by the voluntary consent of several churches convened in mutual command, may declare and determine the mind of the Holy Ghost in the Scripture, and decree the observation of things true and necessary, because revealed and appointed in the Scriptures; which are to be received, owned, and observed on the evidence of the mind of the Holy Ghost in them, and on the ministerial authority of the synod itself' (p.208).

Thus concludes this remarkable piece of ecclesiology. It was written by no armchair theologian but by one who had suffered for his convictions but who in it all was supremely conscious that the crown rights of the Redeemer must never be bartered away.

Notes

[1] William H. Gould (ed), *The Works of John Owen*, XVI, 303-342 (reprinted London, Banner of Truth, 1967).

[2] *Works, XV.*

[3] *Works* XIII, 'A Brief Vindication of Nonconformists from the Charge of Schism as it was managed against them in a sermon preached before the Lord Mayor by Dr Stillingfleet, Dean of St Paul's*', 303-342.

[4] *Works,*XIII. 319.

[5] Ziff, Larzer (ed), *John Cotton on the Churches of New England*, 69-164, 'The Keys of the Kingdom of Heaven' (Cambridge: Harvard University Press, Belknap Press, 1968).

[6] *Works,* XIII. 223, 'A Review of the True Nature of Schism, with a Vindication of the Congregational Churches in England from the Imputation thereof unjustly charged on them by Mr D. Cawdrey"'.

[7] Works XVI. 2, 'Prefatory Note' to The True Nature of a Gospel Church.

[8] *Works*, XV. 223. Subsequent page references will be placed in the body of the text.